Short in the Saddle

And other wild tales of the outdoors

BY DON LAUBACH
AND MARK HENCKEL

ILLUSTRATIONS BY
JOHN POTTER

3 4 5 6 7 8 9 0 CH 07 06 05 04 03

Library of Congress Catalog Card Number 00-133335
ISBN 1-58592-043-6

Published by:
Don Laubach
Box 85
Gardiner, MT 59030

Distributed by:
Riverbend Publishing
PO Box 5833
Helena, MT 59604
toll-free (866) 787-2363

Illustrations by John Potter.

Printed in the U.S.A.

CONTENTS

ACKNOWLEDGEMENTS

In the outdoor world, you're only as good as the people who taught you and the partners who have shared your adventures on streams, rivers, lakes, duck marshes, open prairies and in the high country. They are too numerous to mention, but for all our outdoor mentors and our partners, we give humble thanks. You'll read about many of these friends in the pages of this book. And if we've missed their fondest and most humorous memories in these outdoor tales, it's only because we've been blessed with so many of them.

Some individuals are also worth noting who have contributed their experience, long-term guidance, sense of humor and their ample talents to making the writing this book possible. Among them are Jack Tanner, Warren Rogers, Dick Wesnick, John Kremer, Brett French, Dan Carter, Steve Prosinski, Pat West, Rob Seelye, Art Hobart, Ralph Saunders and an old friend and bowhunting editor, J.R. Absher. Also, Bob Kahle, Jim Stevens, Mark Wright, my brother Doug, Rod Churchwell, Dave Morton, the late Keith Wheat and, last but not even close to the least, the late Gordon Eastman.

Without these folks and many others, we would never even have had a chance to be *Short in the Saddle.*

DEDICATION

To God, who gave us life to do all these things in the
outdoors.

To our guardian angels, who watched over us and helped us
to survive them.

And to our wives, Dee and Carol, who didn't kill us when
we got home and told them what we did.

FOREWORD

Don loves Dee. Mark loves Carol. That ought to be pretty obvious by now. Don and Dee have been married for 42 years. Mark and Carol have been married for 32 years. But before you give us boys a pat on the back for marital longevity, we'll let you in on a little secret. Despite the nuptial bliss, we connived and manipulated our future wives with our wedding days. And we failed at it miserably.

Hunting and fishing were a part of our lives long before these two wonderful and long-suffering women entered the picture. Don grew up on the trout streams and in the elk and mule-deer country of Montana. Mark stalked warm-water fish species and the grouse and white-tailed deer woods of Wisconsin before he headed west.

When it came time for Don and Dee to pick a date to get married, Don balked a bit. It was suggested that May 24 be the wedding date. Oooh, bad choice. It turns out that May 24 was the opening day of the fishing season that year. Don loved Dee a lot. But he loved to fish, too. The wedding date was pushed ahead to May 17.

When his time came, Mark had some input into the wedding date in Wisconsin, too. Hmmm, a fall wedding, eh? Let's look for some dead spots in the hunting seasons. Grouse opened in September. Ducks opened about the first of October. Then pheasants shortly after that. Then the deer season was Thanksgiving week. So how about Oct. 23 as a wedding date? Yup, that's a dead spot between openers. Wouldn't miss any big hunting days with that date.

So we chose to commit ourselves to the loves of our lives at times that wouldn't conflict with our hunting and fishing. Don got married, had a short honeymoon and was still able to get out on the trout streams on opening day. Mark got married and went on a short honeymoon to a part of Wisconsin that was known for its good grouse hunting. Somehow a shotgun got stowed away in the back of the car and he knocked down a grouse on the honeymoon, too. It was Mark and Carol's first meal when they got back home.

But as we said, the fates did conspire against us. We did fail. In Don's case, the opening day of the Montana fishing season was pushed up to the third Saturday in May, which hits on his anniversary from time to time. In Mark's case, he moved to Montana within a year of his marriage and discovered his anniversary sometimes falls on the opening day or in the opening week of the deer and elk rifle season. Curses! Foiled again! Both of us!

Why mention this in the foreword of a book of outdoor tales? Think of it as fatherly advice from two old, long-married guys to the young hunters and fishermen. It's to provide our unmarried readers with some advice on picking a wedding date—and future anniversary date—you can live with for the rest of your life.

If you ever hope to have a rich, full outdoor life when you're married, you can do your best to try to separate love and the outdoors, but even your best laid plans can sometimes go awry. So do the right thing for your future spouse. Pick Christmas Day for the wedding date. They never, ever, open any hunting or fishing seasons on Christmas Day. Plus, you'll save money on gifts so you can buy more hunting and fishing gear for yourself. Just put "Merry Christmas and a Happy Anniversary" on that gift box of wool socks under the tree.

Another good piece of advice is to take extra special care in choosing your spouse before you even decide to say "I do." Then make sure you treat your spouse really well on all the non-opening days of the year.

For all the outdoor things we've been able to do over the years, Dee and Carol understood us and stood behind us. They knew that the occasional fishing or hunting trip might get in the way of an anniversary or a birthday, but we'd try our best to make it up to them the rest of the year. They tolerated us—and loved us. But most of all, they allowed us to do the things we also loved—to enjoy the hunting and fishing, hiking and camping, skiing and boating that fueled a lifetime of tales of the outdoors.

The tales that follow in this book are personal ones—and they're true. As Dee and Carol will assure you, we're definitely not the heroes in any of these stories. Nope, we're not the hero types. We were just lucky enough to go along for the ride with some of our friends and do these things. That's in large part due to two tolerant wives who often kept the home fires burning and the kids bedded and fed while we had a lifetime of outdoor enjoyment, adventures, misadventures and fun. We hope you enjoy reading about them as much as we enjoyed living them. And if you bump into Dee or Carol, give them a pat on the back and tell them that Don and Mark are pretty darn sure they'll be home for their next wedding anniversary—unless, of course, the fish are really biting or the hunting is too darn good.

Don Laubach
Gardiner, Montana

Mark Henckel
Park City, Montana

SHORT IN THE SADDLE

The mountain hunter has never been born who hasn't dreamed of riding horseback into the high country instead of hiking there. For young hunters, it's the long climbs up steep slopes with a heavy backpack that start them thinking equine thoughts. As the hunters age, the climbs get even longer and the mountain slopes seem to get even steeper. By then, the thoughts of horseback hunting become almost unbearable.

If they only had a horse, or maybe two or three. A sure-footed mountain horse would carry them in style far beyond the foot hunters and into new hunting grounds teeming with elk, bighorn sheep and deer. A pack horse or two would allow them to transport a comfortable camp back into the mountains with them, too. Instead of a backpacking tent and one-burner stove, there would be a tent tall enough to stand up in, a big stove to warm the cold nights and dry out wet gear. And, best of all, they could eat real food, instead of that freeze-dried diet. And when the hunter explored his new hunting territory and bagged his trophy animal, he'd have his pack horse to bring that huge elk, deer or bighorn back to civilization.

I had my horse dreams, too. Hunting the mountains since I was old enough to hike in them, I knew the possibilities that mountain horses offered an outdoorsman. I could be a modern day mountain man, exploring the far reaches of the high country in all seasons. I could leave the foot hunters far behind me. I could ride tall in the saddle.

Such are the dreams of the mountain hunter.

But here's the reality of me.

The truth is that I couldn't really afford to buy my own pack string. I had four kids at home who simply wouldn't allow it. They never seemed satisfied to keep their feet the same size so I could stop buying shoes. They wanted to eat three meals each day. My daughter balked at wearing only hand-me-downs from an older brother. My youngest son didn't seem to want to wear his sister's old dresses. So I had to waste money on such frivolous items as food and clothing for the kids. What a blow to the hunting budget!

My hunting partner, Keith Wheat, seemed to be stuck in a similar financial situation. He had his horse dreams, too. But the cost of buying and outfitting and feeding a good mountain horse was beyond his means as well.

That was the why and how of Hernandez.

Hernandez was a four-year-old donkey that came up for sale on a farm on the outskirts of Bozeman. While others blew their budgets on full-size equine equipment, Keith and I shelled out a whole $20 apiece to come up with the $40 asking price for our smallish prize.

On many of the details of his former life, I'm not really sure. We knew he was a breeding jack donkey, had been used to impregnate mare horses, and, hence, he had fathered his share of mules. We knew he was about four years old, had huge ears and big brown eyes. He came with the name Hernandez already in place. That, we heard, had to do with the belief that he was born and probably lived for a time down in Mexico before coming north to our country.

All we knew for sure was that he weighed about 500 or 600 pounds. He was short of leg. He was big of carrying capacity. He was long on personality. And he would make us mounted hunters the next time we headed into the backcountry.

Once we had our donkey, we had to outfit him with saddles and other necessary equipment. To ride Hernandez, I went to a second-hand store and found an old Mexican saddle that had a high back and high horn on it that could be used for riding. Keith, who turned out to be more of the spendthrift in our partnership, then went whole hog and bought a horse. We would make a striking pair when we saddled up to head into the hills that fall. He had his horse. I had Hernandez.

In preparation for that first trip, I rode Hernandez in the pasture where we kept him. It wasn't too bad. He didn't buck. He didn't mind carrying you. He was a pretty good ride. He did have some shortcomings, of course.

By the time I had the stirrups lengthened to fit me, my feet were almost dragging on the ground. That was all right, as long as you watched out for rocks that were sticking up out of the trail or branches that stuck out on the sides. You also had to watch out when you came to a creek. The donkey didn't mind crossing the water, but if I didn't wake up and lift my feet up pretty high, they'd usually get wet. Hernandez was built just too close to the ground to do it any other way.

Our first trip that fall came in September when we headed out to look for bighorn sheep and mountain goats in the Spanish Peaks of south-central Montana. It would take three or four hours to get where we were going. We'd hunt for a time, camp overnight, then return the next day.

The trip was going without a hitch. I rode in on Hernandez while Keith rode his horse. Our gear was distributed between the two, both on the saddles and on our backs. We looked for game all day, but didn't find any sheep or goats nearby. We slept under the high country stars. When it came time to go out the next day, we decided that rather than my trying to ride Hernandez back down those steep trails, we'd put all our gear on the donkey, then Keith would lead his horse and I'd walk out. So we loaded up the donkey, tied the stirrups tight over the top of the gear and we began our descent. Hernandez would just follow along at his own pace.

Partway down, we spotted some mountain goats in the distance and stopped to glass them. We watched those goats for about a half-hour, finally deciding that we didn't want them. In all that time, though we looked at our backtrail often, Hernandez never showed up.

There was little else I could do but to walk back up the mountain after him. I walked about a half-mile and still didn't see him. Finally, when I rounded a bend, I spotted Hernandez peeking around a tree back at me. When I walked up to him, I found out why. It seemed that the donkey hadn't come down the trail after us as we figured he would. Instead, he wandered around out in the woods, feeding on the side slopes, and wasn't really paying much attention to the pack on his back. As a result, the load had slipped to the point that the loaded saddle was now squarely beneath him. Cinched tight, hanging from his belly, and with those short legs, Hernandez couldn't walk a step. His legs were just too short. Once we got him re-packed, he wised up a little and followed us out with no more problems.

On our second trip, those short legs got us in trouble again. This time, Hernandez was our only pack animal so he carried a heavier load. The situation was complicated further by the fact that we were heading in to our hunting spot after dark. The problem came when we started going through some deadfall where there was a big log across the trail. We could step over the log easily. But Hernandez, with his short legs and heavy load, wouldn't even try.

Keith and I each got on one of his front legs and lifted him over the log. Certainly, the donkey would bring his hind feet over himself now. Instead, Hernandez got stubborn. Rather than stepping over, he just laid down on the log and all the urging in the world wouldn't make him budge. And because of the weight of his load, we couldn't lift his rear end over the log, either.

All we could do was take off his load in the dark, then lift his hind end over, and then load him up again. If there was a bright spot to the trip, however, we did get an elk and Hernandez was there, ready and able to pack the elk out a half at a time, while we were set to pack out the camp on our backs. All it would take would be two trips.

Problems of a different kind surfaced on our first trip out. While we were in the backcountry, some other hunters had set up camp into a clearing near the trail. As we came to the spot, we could see their tents and saw their horses picketed out in the clearing. While we didn't pay much attention to it, one of the horses apparently was a mare and if she wasn't receptive to breeding, that wasn't clear to Hernandez.

Some dimly lit memory sparked in the brain of that donkey when he saw that mare. Days gone by when he was in the mule-making business stirred Hernandez's soul. That memory was just enough. The donkey let out a bray. He rolled his lip back. He made a few more strange noises. And half an elk on his back and all, Hernandez headed for the mare picketed right out in the middle of the clearing. He was definitely in the mood for love.

One can only wonder what the mare must have thought. Here comes this strange-sounding donkey, complete with a loaded elk, and apparently heavy in lust. She started jumping up and down. She ran all around the picket stake. For a brief moment, it appeared she wanted nothing at all to do with the donkey. But soon she settled down, and Hernandez seized the moment. He tried to mount the mare to breed her, but with the weight of the elk on his back, Hernandez fell back squarely on his butt. And there he sat. The elk was holding him up now. He couldn't even fall over sideways and try again.

We ended up unloading the donkey again, after we moved the mare to safety. We stood him up and re-packed him one more time. Only this time, we learned to be a bit more careful with our jack when horses were near. It was a stout lead rope and no messing with the mares.

The romantic nature of Hernandez was to be a personality trait that would resurface from time to time throughout my association with him. Those memories of his early days at stud must have been powerful indeed.

I found that Hernandez wasn't exactly particular in his choice of mates, either. I can remember one fishing trip that we made in Yellowstone National Park. It was during the height of the tourist season and we figured that a summer trip into Yellowstone's backcountry would be just the ticket to beat the summer heat and the crowds.

Hernandez was a good and able hand on those summer trips. He allowed us to pack inflatable boats, paddles, and camping gear into remote areas. Without him, we would have been armed only with our fishing rods and the barest of camping essentials.

On this particular trip, we were headed toward Heart Lake with Hernandez safely standing in the back of a pickup truck fitted with a stock rack. The journey would take us about 60 miles on the narrow, winding roads of the park. And, as usual, we ran into tourist traffic jams all along the way. Whenever tourists spotted a deer, a bear, an elk, or a buffalo, they'd hit the brakes on their car and so would everyone behind them. Then the tourists would pour out of their vehicles and risk life and limb trying to get close enough for a snapshot.

We had encountered more than a few minor tourist jams before we finally came to a big one where a herd of elk was grazing in a clearing. So we had to stop. Except this time, Hernandez took note of our stoppage. He peeked through the rails of the stock rack and spotted one of the cow elk. It must have started those erotic memories all over again. He squinted through the rails. His eyes went wide. And he fell in love all over again.

Hernandez let loose with a bray, then another bray, a bellow, and a squeal. He began setting up a ruckus in the back of that truck to the point that the elk didn't know what was going on. For all they knew, they were under attack. The elk started running. The people started running, too. Then some people started climbing trees. Others looked for places to hide. Still others broke for their cars and quickly jumped inside and locked all the doors.

It took a while for people to realize that all the commotion was really coming from just one donkey in the back of our pickup. It was only Hernandez in love. When they realized it, we had a good laugh all around. Cameras that had been so quickly forgotten in the panic of the donkey's braying were back in the tourist's hands. But this time, it was Hernandez who was the focus of their photographic desires.

When we finally made it to the trail to Heart Lake, we were running late from all the delays. We knew that if we were going to make it to camp that night, we'd have to move fast. So we loaded Hernandez with his pack saddle, piled on the gear and cinched it on extra tight. That way, he wouldn't lose it if we had to move quickly.

About halfway in to the lake, we had already crossed numerous small creeks and streams. These waters were small enough that no bridge was required. You just walked over or through the small creek and continued on your way. But, eventually, we came to a bigger stream. This one had what they call a corduroy bridge, constructed of logs. At the end of the bridge where you started to cross, a washout had left a small hole.

As we started to get on the bridge, the donkey stuck his foot in the hole and it spooked him. Hernandez decided the whole bridge must be unsafe. He would go no further. He firmly stood his ground, refusing to budge.

It was a problem. The creek itself looked a little too deep for Hernandez to cross with his short legs. On either bank, swampy ground threatened to mire him down. All we could do was to try to get him to cross on that bridge. I can assure you that we tried every trick known to man to try to get that donkey moving again.

We pulled on his rope. One of us got in front and pulled on that end while the other pushed on his rear. We bent his ear. We called him every name that came to mind. We slapped him on the butt. We tried everything, all to no avail.

Finally, I told Keith that I remembered a long time ago that an old-timer told me that you could always get a donkey to move if you warmed up his butt a bit. I had never tried it, but what else could we do.

I dug some rum-soaked cigars out of one of the packs, lit it up and got it smoking pretty good. Then I lifted his tail up and put the cigar real close to his rump to provide the heat. What Hernandez did, however, was his big mistake and what really got him moving. When he felt the heat of that cigar so close to his butt, he pulled his tail out of my hand and wound up clamping that lit cigar right to his behind.

When Hernandez felt the cigar, he looked me in the eye, then he looked at the bridge, then he did one jump straight in the air and hit the middle of the bridge on all fours. But apparently the cigar was still there smoking because he went up again, did a complete somersault into the creek. That cold water must have woke him up a bit because he let loose of the cigar and headed straight for far bank.

Luckily enough, we got ahead of him and got hold of his lead rope because it looked like he had a notion to head for the tall timber. Standing there, with the fire doused by the creek water, Hernandez allowed us to check our packs. Everything was still in good shape, so we continued down the trail as if nothing had happened.

We had a good fishing trip at the lake. Camp was comfortable, and the fishing was good. But all during our stay, we kept wondering how we'd ever get Hernandez back across the bridge for the trip out.

While at camp, I had smoked up all the cigars. Besides, Hernandez wasn't foolish. He had a memory, too. It was unlikely he'd let me get within a yard of him on the trail if I lit one up there.

Finally, we came up with a strategy that if we only moved quickly enough, perhaps Hernandez wouldn't recognize the spot. If one of us was running fast right in front of him and the other one was running right behind him, maybe we could fool him. .

We started our strategy long before the bridge came into sight. As we got closer and closer to the bridge, we ran faster and faster so that when we finally made it to the corduroy bridge, the three of us were really flying. The strategy worked. Hernandez was across the bridge before he even knew it.

Such were the adventures during the decade or so that Hernandez was my mountain companion. Despite the odd problems, he proved to be a good, if a bit short, equine partner. He was sure of foot. He was tolerant of some precarious slopes. He handled the high country well and took me to places for hunting and fishing that I couldn't have reached without him.

When it came time to retire him, I took Hernandez to my cousin's ranch and turned him loose on some good pasture. He spent the rest of his life there, living into his 20s, and being packed up only occasionally for a trip back to the mountains.

I like to think that Hernandez had a good life there on the ranch. Certainly, he had plenty of time to gaze in the distance and soak in the Montana countryside. He could remember his youth in Mexico. He could recall his lusty years as a breeding jack when the mares were his alone. And, if the day was a hot one, he could think back to a similar summer day on a high country trail when both he and a red-hot cigar cooled themselves with a truly spectacular dive into a cold mountain creek.

THE MUSHROOM PEOPLE

It will be remembered as the night of the mushroom people. Under a blanket of stars in a remote reach of the Montana mountains, the setting was perfect for strange happenings in the night. Of course, even a normal bowhunting camp would appear odd to the casual observer.

Hunters straggle in from the hills after dark, their identities hidden behind faces streaked with the browns and greens of perspiration-run face paint. Lug-soled boots are tugged from aching feet. Sweat-stained hats are lifted off matted hair. Bows and arrows are in evidence at every turn. Amid the scene, hunters settle in to relax around a campfire.

Dinner is in order, and a decent one, for hunters who haven't filled their stomachs since a mangled sandwich was liberated from an odd corner of the backpack and washed down with canteen water eight hours earlier. After all, if you're going to hunt the mountains, you've got to fuel the inner fires.

Hunters must keep their energy level high to cope with rigorous climbs and thin air. They have to light the intestinal burners that will ward off the chill of sleeping out at night. And if a hunter is out in the mountains of September to enjoy a hunting camp experience, he might as well start by making his tummy feel good at the end of the day.

In situations like these, I turn to a hunting partner like Rob Seelye. No rank beginner with a broadhead or a bread-board, Rob's mastery over a two-burner stove is rivaled only by his expertise with bows, arrows and paper targets.

While his prowess on a target range has earned him championship trophies and archery awards, that makes little difference to me come September. He has earned a rightful place in my heart for his bowhunting feeds at the end of a long, hard day.

We had just finished one of those famous feeds of beef-steak buried in butter-browned mushrooms, stacks of fried potatoes, corn on the cob, thickly-buttered bread and fresh milk straight from the cow with the cream still floating on top, when our visitors arrived.

Rob, who once operated an archery shop in Billings during the off-season, yet somehow managed to find someone to man the store during on-season, was stretching out before the campfire for a post-meal beer when headlights suddenly cut through the dark mountain night far in the distance.

Seemingly guided by the rising column of smoke from our fire, the lights headed straight for our camp. Bouncing with the hard-gravel road, swerving right and left with the curves, the lights twisted and turned ever nearer and it was-n't long before a pickup truck rolled in.

Its occupants were two bowmen dressed in camouflage suits much like our own. They sauntered into the glow of the fire and plopped down beside us.

Rob recognized the pair through their greasepaint cam-ouflage masks as hunters he'd encountered earlier on the road and frequent visitors to his shop during the days that led to first weeks of the archery season for deer and elk.

He offered them a beer, which they readily accepted, and we listened to their tales of woe about missed opportunities, stalks foiled by noisy leaves underfoot and shots passed up at does and small bucks because, after all, it was early in the season yet and a big buck would surely be spotted in the long season ahead.

The talk was standard hunting camp fare, and after so many months without that kind of conversation, I settled back away from the fire with my back against a tree to better take in the scene and enjoy the mountain night with a cup of hot camp coffee.

Our visitors explained that they had been up on the high ridges of the Castle Mountains in search of elk for five days,

had stopped here to hunt mule deer today, and were heading for the Yellowstone River near Hysham tomorrow to look for whitetails.

Younger than we were, probably just out of school, and obviously in better shape for such an early-season ordeal, they had logged many miles already on their hunting odyssey and were looking forward to many more ahead of them.

That there were no bucks or bulls to their credit so far was of little consequence. Surely there were trophies just around the next bend in the trail. In the autumn days that remained, there would be many such bends.

During a lull in the conversation, one of them got up and returned to their truck. A little rustling in the front seat and he headed back for the fire, meeting me on the way as I walked toward the glow of the lantern and the coffee pot on the stove beneath it.

In the darkness, between the campfire and lantern, the visitor thrust a paper bag forward and said, "Here! Want one?"

Taking him up on the offer, I stuffed my hand into the bag. Immediately, my hand was met by things cold and clammy inside that dark and mysterious sack. They were slick to the touch, were fleshy, firm and yet fragile, and felt dark, dead and dusty.

Though the visitor was already munching merrily and showed a few teeth to prove that he was smiling, there were doubts about what that bag would offer. What exactly would appear in my fingertips when I withdrew my hand?

Mushrooms?

My questions were answered by the edible fungus in my fingers—a light-colored, whole, huge, fresh mushroom—the kind you pay dearly for in bigger grocery stores.

"Bring that bag over here, I'm starved," his partner called, offering the bag to Rob when it arrived, though in the light of the fire, my partner declined.

"Yeah, we've been living on them for five days. Sure you don't want one? They're really good," the visitor said.

The pair went on to explain that mushrooms were just about all they had been eating since the day before bow season when they set up camp in the Castles. They were the breakfast, lunch, and dinner on which they drew the energy to hunt for miles. They ate only raw mushrooms with a little salt on them, and a few apples, which must have been the balance in their diet.

Strange. Very strange. Considering the negligible nutritional and energy value of fresh mushrooms—which I later looked up in a book and found to be about four calories of energy apiece, give or take a calorie here and there—I had a frightening thought. These men are starving!

They're filling up on fungi that won't give them anything in return. If they keep this up for the entire six-week bow season, and somehow survive, they'll be smearing face paint on sunken cheeks and protruding bones. Their camouflage shirts will be hanging on gaunt shoulders. They'll need to wrap their belts around themselves twice just to keep their pants up. And neither of them will have the strength to draw

Jerky on the Hoof

All wild game meat was not created equal. The best elk meat I've ever eaten came from a six-point bull that I shot in a basin above a hailed-out barley field. The bull had been feeding every night in that barley field for the past month. That meat was a taste delight all winter long. I've had other elk meat that wasn't nearly as good. I have had good deer and not-so-good deer.

But of all the species out there, there's nothing more variable in eating quality than antelope. Good antelope is really, really good. Bad antelope is simply awful.

Jack Tanner got one of those not-so-good antelope one season and by the following year, he decided that his antelope-hunting career was over. I told him if he wanted to hunt, I'd be happy to give him the money for the license. He could apply and get the license. We could go hunting together. He could give me the meat. Jack said that sounded fine to him.

In the months leading up to the hunt, he told me about the not-so-hot eating he had endured the previous year. He promised to shoot me the oldest, meanest, rottenest, toughest, most strong and foul-tasting antelope buck he could find. Jack even gave that antelope a name. He called it "Jerky on the Hoof."

"You just wait until I shoot you Jerky on the Hoof," he'd say. "You'll find out what I mean about antelope meat. Your pronghorn career will be over, too. Just you wait for Jerky on the Hoof."

Jack, my wife Carol and I went antelope hunting that fall. I shot a young buck. My wife filled her tag with a big doe. And then there was Jack. Jerky on the Hoof was an old, old buck. He had heavy fifteen-and-a-half-inch horns. He was big and he smelled pretty strong as we dressed him out, cooled him and put him in the back of the truck for the ride home.

Because that antelope buck was old and likely very tough, Carol and I made the decision to have it all ground into burger. We had it ground with the scraps from the other two antelope and wound up with 55 one-pound packages of antelope burger. We did a test of the meat. We cooked a couple of hamburgers. Woof! They were bad. So then we made a big pot of chili. Chili spices will kill the strong taste. Instead, the strong taste of Jerky on the Hoof killed the chili. Not even the dog would eat that chili.

What to do? We knew nutritionally the meat was good. We weren't going to waste wild game. But how do you make it edible? Another friend, George Shearer, was a home sausage maker. He told me that normally you can't put already-ground meat into a good smoked salami. But what the heck? It wasn't edible now. What did I have to lose? George told me to bring over enough for a small sample batch, about 17 pounds. He'd mix it with one-third pork and add the spices, smoke it and we could give it a try.

That Jerky on the Hoof salami turned out to be excellent. You couldn't have guessed if that salami came from bad antelope or from the finest beef. Even Jack liked it. So we put all the rest of the bad burger into salami, too. Ever since, our antelope meat has become our sausage meat for the year. It's a can't-miss situation. Prime young buck or Jerky on the Hoof, antelope this way provides great eating every year.

back their bows when that big buck finally appears.

So it came as no surprise that they jumped at the opportunity when Rob said there were a couple of ears of corn left on the stove and they were welcome to them. And, have another beer, too. After hearing of their dietary plight, we wished we could have offered them more.

As I leaned against the tree once more, I thought to myself that this pair, now chewing on those corn cobs like two starved pups, were odd ones indeed. Congenial. Knowledgeable about bows and bowhunting. Certainly dedicated and generous and kind and hard-working. But odd, nevertheless. Maybe it was the delirium of starvation. Or, possibly, they hit on the combination of funny mushrooms and apples that were fermented on the tree into skinned cider. Perhaps they were so blasted that they didn't know what they were doing to themselves with that diet.

No, I'm afraid the mushroom people were not like us at all.

As the fire flickered and the night wore on, the mushroom bag was passed back and forth between the two bowmen and the talk continued as they got their daily calories precious few at a time. They told us they were hiking in sneakers now to cut down on the noise because it was such a dry year. Heavy hiking boots would make walking on jagged rocks and unsure footing easier, but they'd put up with the pain. They'd learn to like it.

The mushroom people added that they missed a chance at an elk in the Castles when they slept in one morning because they were exhausted. Sure signs of malnutrition, I guessed. They loved the pain and succumbed to exhaustion.

Big bows and old bowmen, new equipment and stories of strength, accuracy and humor were discussed and laughed about as the moon rose in a pale, yellow ball over the distant peaks. The talk went on and on through another round of beers, the draining of the coffee pot and the demise of the mushroom bag. But it was getting late now, and with a predawn wakeup call for another day of hunting ahead, it was time to turn in.

Instead of having the visiting bowmen hit the road for the Yellowstone at this late hour, Rob suggested that they spend the night in our camp.

"I'm going to sleep in the camper. I've got a bed in there," Rob said, then motioned my way. "But he's got a big tent and there's plenty of room."

Indeed, I had. A four-man, family-sized tent with only one sleeping bag and an air mattress tucked against one wall provided plenty of extra space. A couple of slowly-starving bowhunters would be no problem at all.

"I've got to warn you though," I said in all honesty. "I snore some, especially when I'm tired. And tonight, I'm bushed."

The snoring made no difference at all to the mushroom people. They'd already made up their minds to sleep outside under the stars. Instead of being inside the tent, they rolled out their sleeping bags next to it.

While Rob readied his bed by the light of the lantern, I crawled into the tent and buried myself in a sleeping bag. The last thing I remember was that lantern light casting shadows on the tent wall while one of the mushroom people chuckled at the other's joke.

Nope, they're just not like us at all. Strange, very strange. I yawned to myself as the hiss of the lantern soon became the only sound in that September night in the high country. Mushrooms and stars, apples and sneakers, what an odd, odd . . . . As I drifted off to sleep, I dreamt of long stalks and successful hunts. Restful sleep came quickly in that spacious tent, as the bulls bugled and the bucks snorted challenges and the stars glowed bright against a clear, dark sky.

On the other side of the camp, Rob found the same restful sleep in his pickup camper, fortified against the chill of night by that big dinner and secure in the knowledge that his skills with a camp stove would provide an equally fitful breakfast come morning.

Knowledge that the remainder of our camp wasn't quite so placid came when yellow streaked the eastern sky and the tent shuddered and shook as someone violently began jerking on its tie-downs.

"Knock it off and get out of there," someone snarled as he

jerked on the tent cord. "For Pete's sake, enough is enough!"

Looking out the tent door for the source of the snarling, I discovered that the malcontent was one of the mushroom people, as bleary-eyed and obviously upset at his partner, just a few feet further away from the tent.

"You ... you ... you!," he stammered when he saw me. "You are completely unbelievable. Had I not been here to hear it for myself, I wouldn't have believed it."

"In fact," his partner chimed in, "this whole camp is a little strange. Could you believe the other one?"

As Rob and I looked at each other, perplexed over the vague charges the mushroom people were making, one of them turned on me.

"You said you snored, but that wasn't half the story," he began. "You snorted. You whistled. You wheezed. You grunted. You growled. Then you held your breath, and then started all over again. And you were very loud about it, too, with us lying just on the other side of the tent wall. It was certainly too, too much for anybody to sleep through."

About that time, the other mushroom eater was sauntering over to Rob.

"And about that lantern," he began, pointing to where it still hung from the back door of the camper. "I didn't know you were going to let it burn in our eyes all night. Were you afraid, maybe, that we were going to be attacked by wild animals?"

As the mushroom people jammed sleeping bags into stuff stacks and prepared to leave, Rob and I walked off to compare notes and try to discover the truth about what had obviously angered our visitors. I was exhausted, I admitted, and had probably done my share of freestyle snoring, just one thickness of rip-stop nylon and a few feet away from the pair. Rob said he knew the lantern didn't have much fuel left in it and had decided to let it burn itself out, so it wouldn't leak fuel on the ride home. How did he know it was going to stay lit until 5 A.M., barely a half-hour before we awakened?

As we tried to apologize for what appeared to be our odd behavior, the mushroom people began to laugh. And each time they looked at each other, and then us they laughed a little harder. As they got into their pickup truck to leave, they had both the last word and the last laugh on what could only be described as a strange visitation in the Montana mountains on a September bowhunting night.

"What an odd pair you two turned out to be," they said before pulling away. "You two are odd, odd indeed. One guy makes sounds all night long like a bear getting ready to claw his way out of a tent. And the other one is so afraid of it, he sleeps with a night light!"

RUNNING SCARED IN ALASKA

L et us pause and give thanks that the Good Lord watches over us in our hunting follies. Let us give thanks, too, for the good and trusting people who rescue us and lend helping hands along the way. And, finally, let me give thanks that I don't have to explain one more time to somebody why and how Bob Kahle and I wound up with two untagged dall sheep in our possession and no hunting licenses or money in our pockets.

I can offer those prayers now in earnest—and with a heartfelt chuckle besides—since several decades of life separate me from that first big hunting trip to Alaska. At least, I called it a hunting trip. Bob simply called it Running Scared in Alaska.

The big hunt took place in the late 1960s. Both Bob and I were experienced bighorn sheep hunters in the mountains of Montana, but the lure of new wild places and trophy big game got the better of us. We just had to hunt in Alaska. We'd have to do it on a tight budget, of course. No frills. But what the heck, we were going to go.

We made arrangements with an outfitter who worked the Wrangell Mountains. She assured us that she'd have the hunting licenses, pack stock, gear and an Indian boy to point us in the right direction to find both dall sheep and caribou near the Chisana River. All we had to do was to get to Northway, Alaska, and fly about 100 miles from the Alaska Highway to her camp. She'd have it all ready for us. Who could ask for more? So we packed up our guns and gear in the car at Livingston, Montana, and hit the highway.

That first driving leg of the trip would take us all the way to Dawson Creek, B.C. From there, we climbed on a bus that headed up the Alcan Highway. It would be a 1,200-mile bus trip, broken down into 200- to 300-mile segments where we'd switch buses, grab a bite to eat and continue on the journey. At times, Bob and I were the only passengers riding on the bus and we'd go sit up with the driver and keep him company. Once, a snowy owl took out the windshield of the bus, making for a long, cold ride.

But we made it to Northway and climbed on the little plane that would take us the final 100 miles to a gravel runway near the outfitter's camp. We landed on that runway, thanked the pilot, made arrangements for the plane to return and pick us up seven days later and sent the pilot back.

That's when our hunting license problems began. It seems the outfitter had a fire break out in her camp. All the hunting licenses were burned up in that fire. She assured us that wouldn't be a problem. We could just leave the license money with her and she'd have the next plane that came in go back and pick up licenses for us. She'd have the licenses

waiting for us when we came out of the backcountry with our game. Bob and I pondered that a bit. Hunting without licenses in our pockets? But what could we do? The pack stock was waiting. The Indian boy was there to guide us across the wide and sometimes treacherous waters and soft-sand bottom of the glacier-melt-swollen Chisana River. We headed out for our hunt.

That day, we packed in about as far as we could go, finding a small drainage that led up higher into the mountains and set up camp. Our plan was to hunt that drainage the next day on foot, searching for dall sheep. I had already set my personal goal for the sheep I wanted. I wanted an old ram. It didn't have to be the biggest ram. It didn't have to have the biggest horns. But I wanted an old one.

We got up in the drainage and I spotted a nice ram. I looked him over closely. He was bedded down up in some rock pinnacles. From a distance, he looked good enough to me. I made my sneak up toward the ram and got close enough to give him a good final look as he lay in his bed. He was just what I wanted. So I shot him.

The ram turned out to be an old, old sheep—probably 10 to 12 years old. He slid and rolled down a gravel chute, coming to rest on a little bench. Bob and the Indian boy came over. I dressed the ram out and caped him out. About that time, we heard a helicopter. It was coming up the valley right toward us and finally landed right next to us. A game warden stepped out. It turned out one of our horses got tangled up when it was picketed. The game warden had untangled it and was flying in looking for us just to tell us he straightened out the horses. As long as he was in the neighborhood, he did what wardens always do.

"I would like to see your license," he said. I told him I didn't have any.

"I'd like to see your permits," he said. I told him I didn't have any.

The warden reached into his pocket and pulled out a book. He said, "I'd like you to read sentence 1, paragraph 1." I did. It said you must have in your possession at all times your licenses and your permits.

So I told the game warden our tale of how we arranged for the hunt, how the outfitter said she had the licenses, how the outfitter got burned out and didn't have any licenses and neglected to tell us that until we got there, how we left money with the outfitter to buy the licenses, and how she had said that she would take care of it. The game warden said, "I can't go along with that. I'm going to have to take you boys in and arrest you. You're going to have to pay a fine."

We chatted with the game warden for a while. What else could we do? Finally, he asked us where we were from. We told him it was Livingston, Montana. What a surprise. The game warden was originally from Montana, too. What a small world. We talked for a while longer and the warden finally said he knew we hadn't planned to do anything wrong. We were just the victims of an unfortunate incident. The game warden told us to just get the animals properly licensed when we got back to the outfitter's camp. And he took off.

Bob then had to decide if he was going to try to fill his sheep license. After all the time, all the money, all the effort and working things out with the game warden, there was no reason not to—even if he didn't have a license in his pocket. The warden didn't tell us to stop hunting. He just said to get the proper licenses in place when we returned to the outfitter's camp. So the next day, Bob shot his dall sheep—a truly beautiful ram. It was younger than mine, but had a much better set of full-curl horns.

After enjoying sheep ribs over the fire at camp that evening, we packed back to the outfitter's camp the following day. Still no plane and no licenses. We hunted for caribou the following day and saw a pair of good ones, with great racks, but decided not to shoot them. We had the two dall rams. It was enough.

Still no plane and no licenses when we returned to the outfitter's camp again. This time, we found out that the pilot had contacted the outfitter and told her that his wife had grown ill and the pilot had to fly her to a hospital in Seattle. What he didn't tell her was that he hadn't arranged for anybody else to come pick us up and fly us the 100 miles back to the Alcan Highway to catch the bus. After waiting three more days during which we figured that out, the mail plane finally flew in and we caught the pilot just before he took off.

So I told the mail pilot our tale of how we arranged for the hunt, how the outfitter said she had the licenses, how the outfitter got burned out and didn't have any licenses and neglected to tell us that until we got there, how we left money with the outfitter to buy the licenses, how she had said that she would take care of it, how the pilot's wife got sick, how he didn't make arrangements to get us out, and how we really needed a flight back to where we could catch a bus. The pilot, being a nice guy, said we could finish his mail route with him around the Wrangell Mountains and he'd get us to the bus at Glennallen. We left the sheep with the outfitter, telling her we'd send the licenses and she could ship the sheep out to us in Montana.

After spending the night at a tiny outpost along the way, we found out about flying in Alaska. In the morning, it was fogged in tight. We could see maybe 20 yards. So the pilot held his hand up in front of his face—saw it—and he said, "Sure, we can make it." We flew for at least a half-hour in that pea-soup fog before we could see anything. Then we broke out into the clear. Shortly thereafter, we arrived in Glennallen. We raced to get tickets for the bus, which was due to arrive any minute. And we raced to the bus, heading straight for the driver.

So I told the bus driver our tale of how we arranged for the hunt, how the outfitter said she had the licenses, how the outfitter got burned out and didn't have any licenses and neglected to tell us that until we got there, how we left money with the outfitter to buy the licenses, how she had said that she would take care of it, how the pilot's wife got sick, how he didn't make arrangements to get us out, how we really needed a flight back to where we could catch a bus, how the mail pilot flew us there and how we needed to know if there was anyplace nearby to get licenses for those dall sheep back at the outfitter's camp. The bus driver, being a nice guy, said sure, he knew a place at Tok Junction.

When the bus arrived at Tok Junction, he told all the other passengers to get off the bus and he drove us down several backroads to someone who sold licenses while the passengers waited at a store back by the highway. We got the licenses, picked up the other passengers and continued on the bus back to Northway, to the same airport we had originally flown out of to get to the outfitter's camp.

So I told the guy at the Northway airport our tale of how we arranged for the hunt, how the outfitter said she had the licenses, how the outfitter got burned out and didn't have any licenses and neglected to tell us that until we got there, how we left money with the outfitter to buy the licenses, how

Sardines and Nehi soda pop

Keith Wheat and I did an awful lot of hunting together. We'd go after deer, elk, bighorn sheep, whatever was in season. Sometimes the hunts were for one day, two days, three days, four days. But it seemed like I was always the one who had to figure out the meals. I'd have to plan all breakfasts, lunches and dinners and make sure the food was packed along for all of them. That got pretty old.

Finally, I told myself, "I like sardines. I like Nehi orange soda pop. So why don't I just buy a case of sardines and a case of Nehi and that would be our food supply."

Our next hunt would be a drive-to affair, but it was a long drive to a distant spot in the mountains. We planed to hunt there for about four days, looking for elk. When we arrived, we set up our tent, spread our sleeping bags and arranged our other gear.

Then, Keith asked, "What's for dinner?"

I replied, "Well, all I brought is sardines and Nehi orange soda pop."

"Sardines?" Keith said. "I hate sardines."

I told him that perhaps we could shoot a grouse or two and maybe we'd get that elk we were looking for. That would vary the diet.

The following day took us over an awful lot of country—but none of it had a grouse or an elk in it. We ate sardines and Nehi orange soda pop. The same thing happened the next day. And it happened the next, too.

By the time the trip was over, we'd cleaned up almost the entire case of sardines and all of the Nehi pop. Keith admitted he sort of learned to like sardines on that trip. Of course, we both also smelled like a couple of seals and, in a pinch, we probably could have balanced a ball on our noses, too.

she had said that she would take care of it, how the pilot's wife got sick, how he didn't make arrangements to get us out, how we really needed a flight back to where we could catch a bus, how the mail pilot flew us there, how we asked the bus driver if there was anyplace nearby to get licenses for those dall sheep back at the outfitter's camp, how we got the licenses and how we needed him to get the licenses to the outfitter on the next available plane. The guy at the airport, being a nice guy, said sure, he could get the licenses there.

Bob and I were truly relieved. Finally, our beautiful dall sheep would be legal. We could get on the bus and start our way home. We made it to Whitehorse in Yukon Territory and got a motel room. By then, our cash was running mighty short. There was a place there where we could buy plane tickets to get us back to Dawson Creek and our car, but all I had left was two plain counter checks from the bank back in Livingston. All they had was the name of the bank on them.

So I told the guy who sold plane tickets our tale of how we arranged for the hunt, how the outfitter said she had the licenses, how the outfitter got burned out and didn't have any licenses and neglected to tell us that until we got there, how we left money with the outfitter to buy the licenses, how she had said that she would take care of it, how the pilot's wife got sick, how he didn't make arrangements to get us out, how we really needed a flight back to where we could catch a bus, how the mail pilot flew us there, how we asked the bus driver if there was anyplace nearby to get licenses for those dall sheep back at the outfitter's camp, how we got the licenses, how we needed him to get the licenses to the outfitter on the next available plane, how he said sure, and how we needed to buy plane tickets with a counter check. The guy who sold plane tickets, being a nice guy, said sure, he'd be happy to take our counter check.

It appeared we were on our way once again. We found out it would cost us a dollar each to get from Whitehorse to the airport. We looked in our wallets and set those two dollars aside, then went to the Whitehorse Bar for a brief and cheap celebration of a couple drinks. Everything seemed to be going perfect. The following morning, Bob used his final pennies to buy some peanuts for breakfast and we paid our dollar each to get to the airport.

Once there, we were told that we were allowed one bag for free. We would have to pay extra for all the other bags. What to do now? We were flat broke. I thought for a moment. Then I had an idea. I dug into one of our bags and found some rope. I tied all my bags and Bob's bags together into one huge bundle—a single, giant bag that was so heavy nobody could lift it. As you might imagine, the guy loading the baggage turned out to be a little guy. He came over, took one look the bag bundle, and asked what was going on with this.

So I told the little guy who was packing the baggage on the plane our tale of how we arranged for the hunt, how the outfitter said she had the licenses, how the outfitter got burned out and didn't have any licenses and neglected to tell us that until we got there, how we left money with the outfitter to buy the licenses, how she had said that she would take care of it, how the pilot's wife got sick, how he didn't make arrangements to get us out, how we really needed a flight back to where we could catch a bus, how the mail pilot flew us there, how we asked the bus driver if there was anyplace nearby to get licenses for those dall sheep back at the outfitter's camp, how we got the licenses, how we needed him to get the licenses to the outfitter on the next available plane, how he said sure, how we needed to buy plane tickets with a counter check, how we got the tickets and now were broke and needed to get our bags back home. The little guy who packed the baggage on the plane, being a nice guy, just shook his head and smiled and loaded our giant bag.

We flew to Dawson Creek, got to the airport and found out it was miles back to town. We got a taxi and planned to cash the final counter check at our motel, get enough money to pay the taxi, buy gas for the trip home, and have enough money to even buy food and lodging on the way back to Livingston.

So I told the guy at the motel our tale of how we arranged for the hunt....... Oh to heck with it, you know what I told him. He cashed our check. We paid the taxi driver. We got money for food, lodging and gas. We pointed our car toward home.

On that long drive, Bob told me, "You know, hunting with you is like running scared. You never know what is going to happen on the next turn." And we laughed and laughed.

A year passed and we still hadn't received the sheep horns and capes from the outfitter. So I finally called the Anchorage Chamber of Commerce. I told the person there our long tale of running scared in Alaska, and I asked if he would check for a couple of dall sheep crated up in a warehouse somewhere that never got shipped. The guy called back and said yes, he had found them, but they didn't have any address on where they should be shipped. They had our names on them. So I sent him some money and we finally got the sheep.

As I look at those mounted sheep now, I still have to laugh. It was a great adventure and a hunting trip to remember—Running Scared in Alaska.

MIRACLE ON THE BOULDER

E ven now, I remember it fondly as "The Miracle." And even now, my wife shudders and her skin crawls at the mention of it.

It was certainly a night to re-member in the mountains of Montana—an event of mystical, if not biblical, proportions. It was a scene that I'll probably never wit-ness again—especially if my wife has anything to say about it.

The Miracle took place in late June more than 25 years ago, at a makeshift car camp on the banks of the Boulder River, far above Big Timber and McLeod and the scattered church camps.

My wife Carol, a work friend named Jack Tanner and I were roughing it—and liking it that way. We were, of course, much younger then. We didn't have a camper, a tent or even a tarp. We didn't have much camping equipment at all. But we didn't care. We were happy just to leave our jobs behind, flee the city and get high on the high country.

So we stuffed sleeping bags, cooking gear, some food, a saw, bucket, shovel, lantern, and fishing equipment into the back of my Ford Bronco. Then we jumped in ourselves and hit the road.

The upper Boulder was a perfect destination, perhaps even more perfect than it is for campers and fishermen today. There were the same rough rocks and ruts in the road, some developed and undeveloped camping spots, some deer and the occasional elk and black bear, some rainbow, cut-throat and brook trout. There also were a lot fewer people up there back then.

So we picked a convenient turnout, spun the wheel of the

Bronco into an undeveloped site and settled into camp.

It was beautiful. The crystal clear rush of the stream cascading over water-smoothed rocks competed with bird songs and breezes hushing through the pines for quality time in our ears. The scent of wildflowers and evergreens was exhilarating. The sight of dippers, warblers, and pine squirrels and the deep purple of the snow-capped peaks around us was a treat for the eyes.

After an early dinner, Jack and I grabbed our fishing rods and headed for the river for an evening of uncrowded angling. I've always felt that the Boulder River somehow epitomized everything a Rocky Mountain trout stream was meant to be. It's ice-cold. It's gin-clear. The froth of its riffles is pure white. Its pools are deep green-blue. You can count the rocks on the cobblestone bottom, except where they disappear into deep, mysterious pools.

I can remember the time when I shared one of those pools with a mountain beaver. It waddled along the bank toward the pool, then slid in. The beaver swam in circles in front of me, before hitting the water with its tail in a quick dive that sounded like someone tossed a giant boulder into the pool. Then he came up and did it all over again. And again. And again. It was a prolonged close encounter with an animal you rarely see at that close range. It was an experience to remember.

Come evening in June, as it was right now for Jack and me, you always see some type of insect flying over the waters of a stream like this. You always have some trout dimpling the surface with rises. But on this June evening, the trout were especially active.

Bigger trout were tearing up the water just below the riffle and tight along the far bank. Smaller trout at the tail of the pool were equally aggressive. It was as strong a show of rises as I'd ever seen on this river. And rarely do you see the trout slash the water like this so consistently. Something was really sparking a strong feeding spree.

As a relative novice at the fly fishing game back then, I looked to the skies above the stream and saw only a few bugs there. Some were light green. Others were minuscule and brown. Neither looked like anything in my fly box. I looked at the surface of the water and didn't see much there, either. Just a few, scattered, teeny, tiny bugs.

Without much for guidance, I started methodically going through my flybox trying first this, then that. Jack did the same.

I whipped and flailed the waters with a flyboxful of patterns that evening, turning the session into a couple of hours of casting practice while the trout merrily went on their feeding spree in spite of me. All I caught was one tiny rainbow. Trout splashed all around my offerings, but ignored them all the same.

But, what the heck, the scene was exquisite anyway. The weather was as perfect as a cool mountain evening can get. The backdrop was beautiful. I was fishing. And I was high in the mountains, far from work and phones and too many people. If I didn't get the trout tonight, maybe I'd get them tomorrow morning.

By the time the moon rose over the peaks, Jack had wan-

dered back to camp from his fishing and started a campfire. Carol and I found a comfortable sitting log nearby. We settled in for an evening of pleasant conversation, a beverage or two and a chance to soak in more of the beauty of a night on the Boulder.

It wasn't too far into our conversation when I felt something crawl up the back of my neck. It was a bug, and I quickly brushed it away.

A few minutes later, another bug crawled up my neck—brush. A few minutes later, there was another—brush, brush. Then Jack felt something. Then Carol. All of them bugs—big bugs.

What was going on? What was with all the bugs all of a sudden? Grabbing the lantern, I held it high to spread its light on the ground around us. Here and there in the light of the lantern, I saw more bugs on the ground around us.

Wow! Salmonflies! It was, indeed, a miracle.

Scattered around us, crawling away from the stream, were big salmonflies. These giant members of the stonefly family crawled out of the stream as nymphs minutes ago, broken out of their hard shells and emerged as insects fully as big around and as long as your little finger.

Those insects were now looking for things to crawl up on, so their wings could dry, so they could find mates, so they could fly out over the water the following day and deposit the eggs back in the stream.

It was a miracle!

I was exhilarated. I was inspired. I had seen the unique fabric of nature unfold before me, which God had so intricately woven.

In short, I had seen the bugs, if not actually the Light.

And I was up and preaching about it. In the flickering light of the campfire, I spoke with the inspired conviction of a born-again fly fisherman as I told my wife and friend about the miracle that was taking place that night right before our eyes.

I told them about how the big bugs were emerging. I told them the life cycle of a stonefly and that a salmonfly is really a giant stonefly, that glorious *Pternarcys californica*. I told them about how eggs that would be deposited back in the stream by these bugs the following day would hatch into nymphs that would live in the stream for three years.

I told them about how these bugs crawling around us had to escape the jaws of fish and birds for those three years and had survived to be with us this night, crawling out of the river to reach full adulthood to perpetuate their species.

I waxed poetic about the miraculous mystery of creatures of the water that were being transformed into creatures of the land. Three years of living under water for just one night and a day of life in the air. The Holy Grail of fly fishing anglingdom—the salmonfly—was emerging all around us. Most miraculous of all, we were so fortunate that we were actually there for this one marvelous night. After all, it only happens once in a year, only on a stretch of perfectly clean stream, only when the time and the water temperature is exactly right. Then, the miracle happens.

It was a miracle! And I preached on and on about it—the gospel of the salmonfly.

As long as we had a born-again experience going, I also bowed my head and confessed that my failures at fly fishing that evening had been a result of my hopeless ignorance and lack of faith. While I was fishing small dry flies, the trout were gorging themselves on huge nymphs. Had I only had faith in those big black nymphs in my fly box, my fishing would have been saved, fresh trout would have been delivered and our frying pan would have overflowed with the multitude of my catch.

At first, my wife and friend showed some interest in hearing about the miraculous hatch of the salmonflies. But as my sermon went on, despite all my enthusiasm, preaching and grand gestures in the firelight, things got quieter and quieter around the campfire.

When I looked over at the pair, I realized that they weren't smiling anymore. They weren't particularly interested in hearing any more about this at all. In fact, they wore expressions best described as faces full of worry and horror, rather than of excitement and wonder.

Each new bug that they spotted scurrying in the firelight

put another wrinkle on their brow. Each new bug that crawled on them forced a shudder. And my wife periodically shivered, uncontrollably, as if her skin crawled.

Miracle? Salmonflies? Horror?

Carol and Jack, who were obviously much more perceptive to the world around us than I was, then reminded me that we had no camper, no tent and no tarp. In just a few minutes, we'd be spreading our sleeping bags out on that very same patch of ground which was now the home of climbing, crawling bugs—big ones, too—which promised to crawl over us, around us and upon us all night long.

With the frequency we were seeing those bugs, there was all likelihood that come morning, we would not be alone in

Hit like a truck

Some fishing partners have you in stitches all day long. They're just funny, funny people. And, they really know how to tell a tale. John Greene, of Livingston, is one of those people. He told me this tale and swore was true.

It's all about how tough big trout are and how hard they can strike a fly or lure. John said that may be true, but you should still be extremely skeptical of anyone who tells you that a trout they caught hit like a truck.

John said he was fly fishing for trout in Yellowstone National Park some years ago, working a stretch of the Firehole River that ran right along the road. He was casting his fly to working fish and doing pretty well with the trout, as droves of tourists drove past on their way to see Old Faithful and all the other popular spots in Yellowstone.

At this particular time, he was trying to reach a nice trout that rose far across the river and was working the line out, casting forward and back, forward and back, when a Volkswagen drove past on the road behind him. The monofilament leader on his fly line wrapped around the radio antenna of that passing Volkswagen and when the line went tight, it jerked him around in an instant and just about ripped his arm out of the socket.

"It was a good thing that the leader broke," Greene said. "If not, I probably would have been dragged clear to New Jersey.

"But the real lesson of this story is that fishermen tend to exaggerate and lie a lot," he said. "When somebody tells you that a big trout hit like a truck, do not believe them. I can tell you personally that trout not only don't hit like a truck, they don't even hit like a Volkswagen."

our sleeping bags.

Miracle? We stayed up around that campfire for a long, long time that night. We hunted for more wood by lantern-light to fuel the campfire several times. Sometime past mid-night, we finally spread out our sleeping bags, but not before spraying two full cans of insect spray on the ground around us, hoping that it would do for the salmonflies what it does for mosquitoes. Nervously, we settled in for the night.

As I recall, we were alone in those sleeping bags in the morning. We had a good bit of luck fishing that following day, too, taking our cue from the salmonflies we'd seen in the firelight.

After the night of the miracle, it might have been the end of mountain camping for my wife. She hates bugs—even lit-tle ones—that much. But my wife surprised me. In all hon-esty, it really didn't take too long at all before my wife agreed to go camping again up in those beautiful mountains, beside the beautiful waters of the Boulder River.

It happened just as soon as I broke down and bought her a solid, secure, bug-proof tent—and a couple more cans of insect repellent, just in case.

PITY THE PARTNERS

Yes, I've been bad—very, very bad. And if I wasn't laughing so hard every time I think about being so bad, I'd be ashamed of myself. But, such is the life for greenhorns and partners in this country. When you put them in the company of experienced hikers, hunters, campers or fishermen, the new guys tend to get the worst of it. And I'm guilty—chuckle, chuckle—of doing my share of being very, very bad to them.

For example, I used to do a lot of fishing on the Madison River. The Madison is a spectacular trout fishery—one of the world's finest. But it's also home to countless other fish and wildlife species. It happens to be sprinkled with moose, too.

One day, Jim Stevens, my brother-in law, and I were fishing on the lower part of the Madison when I went through a bunch of willows. I found a young bull moose there and, to get him out of my way, began throwing rocks at him. The moose didn't like that too well and began chasing me around a bit. I finally climbed up a fallen cottonwood and got fairly high.

I saw Jim coming along and he hollered at me, asking what I was doing up in the tree. I said I climbed up there to see if I could find a rabbit. I had spotted it in the willows and was throwing rocks at him. So Jim decided to help. He started into the willows to help me find that rabbit. When he got in there, the moose saw him coming. That spooked the moose. It also spooked Jim.

What happened next would have made many a football running back coach proud. Jim busted out of the willows like he was headed through line with the moose hot on his heels. Jim, wearing waders and carrying a fishing rod, then cut a zig-zag course across the meadow. Jim cut to the right.

Jim cut to the left. Wow! What a broken-field runner! He could really run fast in those waders! No wonder he was a track star in high school. That boy could really move.

Jim never looked back. If he had, Jim might have noticed that the moose wasn't zig-zagging with him. The bull was just running straight. Meanwhile, Jim's course kept putting him at risk, every time he turned he cut back in front of the moose.

It was a good thing that the moose really wasn't after him. The moose was just trying to get away from us. Finally, Jim stopped. He ran out of steam and simply couldn't run any-more. The moose continued on, roaring past him toward the security of another patch of willows just ahead.

As for me, my big success was in not falling out of my cottonwood tree. That wasn't easy. I was laughing so hard as the scene unfolded that my sides ached and my arms grew weak until I finally couldn't laugh anymore. What a gallop toward the safety of an imaginary end zone! Go, Jim! The entire squad of the Green Bay Packers would have stood up and

cheered for him that day. As for me, I just couldn't stop laughing—and I laugh even now every time I think about it.

Another memory that always makes me laugh involved my friend Mark Wright, back when he was greenhorn in the high country. Mark was a flatlander, a common non-mountain creature whose native habitat lies in the eastern portions of the United States. But Mark was trying to become a mountain creature, like my brother Doug and me.

A big, strong kid with a good sense of humor, Doug and I had victimized Mark early on during a trip into the high country. We hired an outfitter to carry our gear to camp on horseback. Mark knew that, but apparently didn't know exactly what that was all about. Our packs looked full, so Mark packed his gear into his backpack. Doug and I cruised the trails easily that day, while our young friend huffed, puffed and struggled on the trail. "Breaking in a flatlander," I told Doug, loud enough that Mark could hear it. "Those flatlanders just can't take it." When we arrived in camp, we pulled fluffy light clothing and jackets out of our packs. Mark knew he'd been had.

By the time we planned another trip—this one to hunt bighorn sheep—Mark knew the ropes. He loaded his heavy backpacking gear onto the horse just like Doug and I did. On that trip, we hiked in 17 miles to where the horses had dropped off our gear.

We told each other this trip would be strictly for bighorn sheep. No elk would be shot. If we shot an elk, we'd have to hike all the way back out to get horses to pack the meat back to civilization. A couple days into the trip, Mark and I were hiking together while Doug had taken a different route. Our plan was to meet him up on top of a ridge.

Doug arrived there first and found a little toy flute up there that some other hunter had left behind. The flute made just one note. But it sounded something like the high-pitched whistle of a bugling bull elk, which is why the previous hunter had packed it up there.

From his position up high, Doug could see Mark and me working our way up through the rocks. So Doug hid behind a log and blew on the flute. My eyes lit up. So did Mark's. I looked at him and said, "Elk!" So in spite of the rules, we both loaded a cartridge into the chamber of our rifles and started our sneak up toward where the sound was coming from. Pretty soon, we hear this voice. "So you guys aren't going to shoot any elk, eh?" Doug said. We lied. "No, we were just coming up to take a look." Doug replied, "Then why did you guys load your rifles—just to take a look." We all laughed. Doug knew he had us. We did, too.

Doug and the Bear

My brother Doug and I were always doing a lot of hiking in the backcountry, looking for lakes to fish. Fishing and summertime went hand in hand, and the prospect of finding a good new lake always excited us.

Such was the case with a little lake we heard about that was supposed to harbor some huge trout. The location of the lake, however, was a little sketchy. We looked at various maps trying to locate it and thought we had it pinpointed pretty well. We just couldn't tell if it was back in the timber or out on the edge of the timber.

So we hiked into the area where we thought it should be and walked about 200 yards apart from each other—Doug back in the timber a ways and me out on the edge. As I was walking along the edge of the timber, I spotted a black bear sleeping. He was sleeping hard.

I decided to make a sneak on him and then wake him up. I had an aluminum fishing rod tube with me. The rod was inside, but it didn't have a cloth cover on it. When I got fairly close, the bear was still asleep. So I started shaking that rod tube up and down. Each time the rod hit the end cap, it would make a loud popping sound.

That bear awakened with a start. He was real surprised. His eyes got wide, and he took off at a dead run—right in Doug's direction. Doug, for his part, was real surprised, too. First, there was this loud popping sound. Then, there was this black bear racing straight at him. He thought he was being charged.

In an instant, Doug dove for a tree and started clawing, scratching and climbing as fast as he could. The bear never even gave him a look. He raced past the tree and off into the forest.

I thought it was all pretty funny, except for the lake part that came later. Our prime trout lake turned out to be nothing but a shallow mud hole full of axolotls—sometimes called mud puppies. No trout. No fishing. Just Doug and his bear as a memory we still laugh about often.

No bighorn sheep were shot on that trip. After the fourth day, it was time to pack up our gear and head out. We opted not to have the outfitter and horses come back for our equipment. All we had was the sleeping bags, tent and a few other items to pack out.

Mark was all packed and had left camp to get a drink out of the creek when Doug hatched an evil plan. Doug gathered up three pretty good-sized rocks and buried them in Mark's pack, under the clothes and other items. When Mark came back and slung on his pack, he commented that the pack felt a little heavier. We assured him it was just his imagination.

As I said, Mark was a big, strong kid, but he worked up a pretty good sweat under the burden of that pack as we hiked the 17 miles out. Each time he mentioned the weight of that pack, I'd tell him, "Yeah, you're just a flatlander and can't take it like Doug and I can. It makes a difference when you're born to the mountains. You flatlanders can't even hold up on a little hike like this one."

As often happens after a trip, when we got back to town, the backpacks aren't emptied right away. After all, we wouldn't need them until the next trip. Why rush? This time, about a month went by before Mark showed up with lightning in his eyes. He came up to Doug and me and he was screaming at us. "Who put the rocks in my backpack?" Mark demanded. Come clean? Not us. Doug and I both denied any knowledge of the answer to his rock mystery.

But to this day, we laugh about it. And also to this day, we check our backpacks very carefully before we hoist them onto our shoulders. Someday, we knew our flatland partner would get even. But it hasn't happened—not yet anyway.

BULL MOUSE AND BULL MOOSE

There's no justice in those highly prized hunting licenses—none at all. The rich get richer. The poor get poorer. And most of us find out we're license-poor in the long run.

Forget about an even break when it comes to fatherhood, too. That also is as rare as a mountain mongoose at snow snake time. And when it comes to luck ... how's that old saying go? ... If it weren't for bad luck, I'd have no luck at all.

Grim testimony to these facts all came to pass during one fateful hunting season some years ago. In fact, that season has been indelibly marked in my memory as the year of bull moose and the bull mouse.

It all started in August when some mail arrived in our post office box—and some mail didn't. You don't have to be a western big game hunter for too many years before you learn about the drawing system of awarding big game licenses.

In our home state of Montana, for example, any resident can hunt deer. You just buy the license over the counter at the local sporting goods shop or other state license agent. A resident can buy a general elk license, too. And, if you want, you can buy a black bear license over the counter, as long as you've passed your bear identification course.

But to get the really juicy stuff—the limited-entry, high-percentage elk hunting districts with the biggest bulls, the elk cow permits, the antelope tags and, perish the thought, licenses for bighorn sheep, mountain goats or moose—you've got to be lucky in the annual drawings.

It's a case of fill out the applications, mail in your money and pray for a couple of months until the state revs up its computer—that dratted computer—decides who's lucky and who's not, and spits out the licenses. Thereupon, you camp out at your mailbox on the fateful day they're due to arrive and hope your hunting prayers were answered.

For the first 18 years I was a resident of Big Sky Country, I did all those things—especially the praying. I filled out the applications. I mailed in my money. And I prayed—Lord, did I pray. I then camped out at my mailbox. But other than some antelope tags in districts where everybody who applies gets one, my license prayers went unanswered.

No sheep tag. No goat tag. No moose tag. None of those big bull elk tags, either. That kind of track record should earn me the title of King of Rotten Luck.

Enter my 13-year-old son, Prince Andrew the Obnoxious. Wet behind the ears. Green as grass. Looking at just his second hunting season. How did the computer gods look at this?

First, he got a second deer tag and an antelope tag.

"Isn't that what's supposed to happen, Dad?"

Then, he got a highly coveted cow elk rifle permit in the Missouri Breaks.

"You send in your money and they send you the tag—sounds simple enough."

Finally, he hit the jackpot. In a hunting district that awarded just two bull moose permits for the year, he drew one of them.

"Never got one of these yourself, huh? It doesn't seem that tough to get a moose permit to me. How come you never got one? It's easy."

That pretty much sealed my fate during the rifle season. I probably wouldn't get much hunting done myself. But I'd be extremely busy as a dirt road taxi driver, ferrying my son around on all these glamorous hunts.

Ah well, at least there's the bow season, I thought. Andy will be too busy with football to do much bowhunting. I'll get my big bull elk during the bow season. That might take the edge off of my failures in the drawings. No problem. We'll bag that big bull elk with an arrow. That will put the prince in his place.

With two full weeks of vacation to play with and a campsite located in an area known for big bulls, it ought to be a snap. The Montana archery big game season became something of a focus for me during those last weeks of summer. I practiced with my bow and arrows every day. I set up my tent trailer in advance of the season. I helped put up tree stands. I cut shooting lanes. I watched bull elk and dreamed about the one that would walk within range while I was on stand or the one that I'd call up when I hiked the slopes.

Funny how things work out. When the season arrived, instead of bull elk, my two-week hunt was filled with bull mice. There were mice everywhere that year—big ones. They were so big, about the only thing the bull mice didn't have was antlers.

I found this out when I arrived at the tent trailer on the day before the season opened. I don't know how they got in, but I found the mice had moved into its storage compartments for the winter. They lived in the drawers. They had stacked a winter supply of seeds against the interiors of the wheel wells. Mice were everywhere.

My daily routine was set by the following day. In the mornings, I'd hike the hills and hunt. In the afternoons, I'd return to the trailer to battle the mouse invasion in hopes of evicting my rodent companions. Then I'd hunt on stand for elk in the evenings. There was nary an elk to be seen. But the mice came out in force to scurry back and forth in the leaves beneath my stand—so loud on the forest floor that I couldn't have heard an elk approaching if there had been one on its way in. Finally, at night, I'd fall asleep to the sounds of the next wave of mice in the trailer renewing their invasion and replenishing the food caches that I'd thrown out in the afternoon.

After two weeks, I had endured quite enough of the camp on what became known as Mouse Hill. I had no bull elk. I hadn't even gotten a shot at a bull elk. But it was time to take the young prince into the mountains for moose.

In retrospect, it would be nice to say that the kid suffered for a long, long time from the same misfortunes I did—a severe lack of target—and it was only through my keen eyesight and bountiful knowledge of the wilds that he eventually filled his tag. But, in truth, it took him only two days with Don Laubach to get a three-year-old bull. I wasn't even with him when he did it. Andy and Don hiked me into the ground on the first day out. So instead, he was with Don when they spotted the moose on the morning of the second day. Andy nailed it perfectly with the first shot. And, to top it all, it went down within 75 yards of a logging road covered with just enough snow that an outfitter friend was able to drag it easily to the trailhead with just one saddle horse.

It was a terrible way that boy bagged his bull moose. The boy didn't suffer. Just how terrible, I began to find out on the way home.

"You didn't really deserve that tag," I told him. "I've been putting in for years and years for a moose tag and I've never drawn one."

"I've been putting in for years and years too, Dad—two of

them," Andy replied. "You know Dad, you're really lucky I'm such a nice guy. I let you come along and be my moose hunting apprentice and pay for all this for me."

At that, he laughed. He seemed to be enjoying it, so he continued.

Holding up his right hand, he remarked, "You know, this is the perfect trigger finger—I bet you wish you had one like it. One shot. One moose. Maybe I should have the finger bronzed." There was more. He began singing what he called Christmoose carols like, "I'll be home with Christmoose, you can count on me, but not my Dad because he never draws a tag...."

Andy began preparing for his week back in school asking me about different ways he might casually work the word "moose" into the conversation.

"How about telling my football buddies, 'Wow! You really hit that guy like a moose. By the way, did I tell you about the moose I got and how I allowed my dad to touch it . . . ?' Or maybe, 'Are you headed for Moose class, I mean Music class? I'm really good at being a moose hunter, so it's on my mind. My dad wouldn't know a moose if he met it on the street because he can't even draw a tag....'"

The boy was needling hard. And there were no signs of slacking off even after we got home. In fact, his favorite saying, which he repeated to everyone within earshot, was "You know it's awful tough when you're only 13 years old and you have to provide for your family because your dad can't do it." Then he'd laugh and laugh—that obnoxious, teenage, snot-nosed-kid-laugh of his.

Needless to say, there wasn't much ammunition I had at my disposal with which to do battle with him. You can only stretch a bull mouse so far in trying to call him a trophy. And the tale of how you evicted one from your tent trailer sounds pretty much like the way you evicted all the rest. What kind of glory is there in saying, "Yup, I was smarter than the average mouse."

The only solace I have is that the law of averages can't help but catch up with Andy. He'll join the thousands of other hunters who wait and pray for those permits only to come up empty year after year after year.

I told him that, too. But Andy didn't quite see it that way.

"It's okay if we don't put in for a moose permit next year, Dad," he told me. "I'm going to apply for something else. Maybe I'll even let you be my apprentice when we go

The Big Buck Antelope Contest

Nope, I'm not much of a trophy hunter. Neither is Ralph Saunders. But nothing holds us back from wagering on our annual two-man "Big Buck Antelope Contest." The stakes are huge—the loser buys the winner lunch.

It's truly a contest to behold. One year, I won the big buck contest by shooting a doe. Another year, Ralph was cutting up the meat and had thrown his antelope head in the garbage because it was so small, but figured he probably should measure it anyway. He won that year by two inches. I won one year when I didn't get an antelope, but drew an antelope tag. Ralph had forgotten to apply. Another year when neither of us got an antelope, the loser was decided by who missed more often. I think I won 2-1. Or did Ralph win that year? It doesn't matter.

Perhaps the most fun with this contest comes in the weeks and months leading up to the antelope season. That's when we call each other on the phone and try to invent new contest rules.

Ralph has a good hunting spot about 50 miles from Billings. My spot is 150 miles away. Shouldn't I get an extra inch or two on the horns because I burn more gasoline getting there?

I pretty much always remember to put in for a license. Sometimes Ralph gets busy and forgets to put his application in the mail. Shouldn't Ralph get extra points when he actually remembers to apply?

Ralph's son, Lonn, is an airline pilot. Ralph should get points taken off because he's got Lonn scouting from the air for him—even if he is scouting from real high, going real fast.

I've usually got one or both of my sons hunting with me who are willing to drag my antelope back to the truck. Ralph often hunts alone, so he can't shoot a real big buck for fear he can't drag it back to the truck himself. That means my bucks should have inches subtracted from their horns.

Nope, it's really not too serious a contest. But we wouldn't have it any other way. We do have an awful lot of fun with it—even in the years when the winner forgets to collect on his free lunch.

bighorn sheep hunting instead."

MOUNTAIN RODEO

Pack stock is often a blessing. Sometimes it's a curse. Always, it's an adventure. Depending on who you talk to, the horses and mules that mountain hunters use to pack into the backcountry can be the greatest of helpers or the worst of nuisances.

That's one of the reasons why I've always had great admiration for the good and true mountain outfitter—the one with the solid string of horses and mules that carry people and gear beyond the reach of the legs of mortal man. The good outfitters have good stock and good people handling their stock. The horses and mules are in good shape. They're gentle on the riders and solid with their packs. Done right, a pack string will get you in, and get you out, even in the worst of weather. They've saved the hides of many who have ventured into the high country in search of fish and game.

But even with good stock, you can have your mountain rodeos. Ask any outfitter or any experienced pack stock hunter and he'll have more than a few tales of tangles and tight spots, rodeos and wrecks on high, mountain trails. That's why it's always—let's just call it interesting—when you introduce new pack stock to the mountains.

That was the situation I found myself in late one fall in the high country near my home in Gardiner, Montana. I was lucky enough to draw a bull moose permit that year—a rare and precious draw for any hunter here. But the hunting season was quickly slipping away on me.

There was just about one week left when my cousin noted that the season was rapidly running out and the snow was beginning to pile up in the mountain drainages. We both had elk licenses left, too, as did some of our friends. We decided to have one last big hunt in the high country. My cousin, who ranched near Big Timber, would bring the horses. We could set up a mountain camp. If we were real lucky, we just might find a moose yet to fill that tag.

So the trip came to pass in the Bear Creek drainage. My cousin and friends loaded the pack stock and saddled their horses. I was the one who got to hike in and lead the new mule. This young mule had never been packed into the mountains before. He was a good, solid animal, my cousin assured me, but he was green as grass. It would be up to me to teach him the ropes.

With the rest of the party still packing gear, I began my hike in with the loaded mule, figuring the other hunters would catch up to me soon enough. I had gone about a mile up the creek bottom when the first rodeo broke out. The mule decided he didn't like that pack on his back and he started bucking and kicking. High and wild, that young mule kicked snow in all directions as the pack on his back became looser and looser and finally began shedding its contents. By the time the mule was done, sleeping bags and other assorted gear were strewn far down the slope. I got the mule tied up and started gathering up our scattered equipment, deposited far and wide in the snow. I packed the mule back up again with the help my friends who had, by that time, caught up to me. The pack string moved on.

About a half-hour before we got to camp, we spotted a couple of bull elk in a distant clearing, which offered promise for the following morning. But when we got to that spot the next day, all we found were tracks, which we followed back to within 50 yards of our camp and continued on up the creek drainage. The bull elk had passed us sometime in the night or early morning and kept on going. While the other hunters kept on the trail of the bulls, a friend and I hiked toward the head of the drainage, following a creek bottom in hopes of finding a moose. As we moved up the creek, the snow began getting deeper, to the point where we finally had to put on the snowshoes we had packed along just in case.

It was up near the head of that creek that we spotted a bull and cow moose. With so little time left in the hunting season, that bull looked like a trophy to me. No time to be picky. But just as we spotted them, the bull and cow moose spotted us and lit out up the slope. Have you ever seen a couple of hunters trying to run on snowshoes in pursuit of moose? It can be done. It's sort of a splayed-leg, high-kneed, feet-go-wide, ugly sort of running. A lot of snow gets kicked up in the process. The snowshoed runners look like they're about to crash at any moment. In short, it isn't pretty. You also can't run the four-minute mile in snowshoes, or, in my case, even the fourteen-minute mile. But ugly runners that we were, my friend and I were able to cover ground quickly enough that I got a shot at that bull moose as he headed up-slope about 100 yards away. A single shot brought him down.

Hearing the shot, my cousin and friends found us. It was

hearty congratulations and celebration all around. A hunter just doesn't get a moose every day—or even every year. For many, it's the trophy of a lifetime. So there was good reason to celebrate. I skinned out the moose to make a moose rug, split the quarters for packing and in a couple of trips, we had it all packed back to camp.

That night, the celebration continued around the campfire. We had a hearty dinner that fortified our bodies and had packed along some spirits to boost our....well, our spirits. We talked and laughed and drank. Then we drank and laughed and talked. At some point along the way, someone got to talking about mountain rodeos with pack stock. I don't know for sure who came up with the idea, but we decided to hold our own rodeo right then and there. No doubt, the spirits helped us along in our decision.

In a snowy clearing in the moonlight, we decided to hold our own mule-riding contest with that young, new mule that we had brought along. Mule-riding rules? It was simple. This wouldn't be a one-rider mule-riding contest. It would be a two-rider mule-riding contest. As one guy held the mule steady and another held the mule rope, the two mule riders climbed on. None of the early riders lasted more than a second or two. By the time it came around to my turn, one of the smaller hunters among us was holding the mule rope. And, like the others, my partner and I were dumped quickly, except this time, the young mule took off running, dragging that little hunter through the snow of that clearing like a snow-plowing toboggan. He held on for as long as he could, but finally had to let go. Off and away, the young mule kicked and bucked and raced off into the darkness, trailing his rope behind him.

There we were. It was the middle of the night. We were laughing and snow-covered and certainly well spirited. And now we had a runaway mule on the loose. How were we ever going to find him and get him back? Finally, it came to me— caramels! After that rodeo on the trail as we hiked in, I found that young mule had a horrible sweet tooth for caramels. Every time things looked like they were going to get a little rough, every time it looked like I might have a rodeo, I'd give the mule a caramel and it would settle him down. Why not try it? What do we have to lose?

With each of the hunters shaking a little plastic bag of caramels, we fanned out from camp in search of the mule. And, believe it or not, the tactic worked. The young mule finally came wandering out of the black timber, drawn by the sound of rattling caramels and with bright eyes that his sweet tooth was going to be rewarded. After a caramel or two or three, we led him back to camp and tied him up for the night.

Our group never did take any elk on that hunting trip. For the most part, the rest of the hunting was pretty uneventful. We had learned our lesson when it came time to pack out of the mountains and decided to go easy on that young mule. We'd use a more experienced packhorse to carry the moose head and hide back out to the trailhead. No use risking yet another rodeo with that young mule.

Packed up and ready to go, we headed down the trail toward home and had gone about a half-mile when we came to a clearing, the wind began to pick up, and that experienced pack horse glanced around to see what was on its back. Its eyes got real big as it saw that moose hide ruffling in the wind, and it instantly went into orbit.

That horse bucked and kicked and spun and flailed for another half-mile down a steep slope, scattering the moose hide, my personal gear, spotting scope and other equipment all along the way. The only thing that stopped him was that his back leg got stuck between the pack saddle cinch and his body and he crashed into a tree. When we got there, the horse's eyes were still bugged out and we thought he was dead. But after we cut the cinch and got his leg out, the horse simply got up and began shaking.

Once again, we began picking up gear. A duffle bag of mine was now a strip of fabric 10 feet long and two inches wide. I combed the spot looking for lost gear and still didn't find it all. All we could do was re-pack the horse and hide the moose hide from the horse's view and head on down the trail.

Mountain rodeos are just part of the game when you head into the high country with horses and mules—whether you plan the rodeos yourself over a campfire, or just let them happen on their own.

KILL THE WEATHER GUY

Murder is such a harsh word. So is the phrase, hang by the neck until dead. Yet they seemed so appropriate when applied to a certain unnamed weather forecaster at a small Montana radio station His was the cheerful voice, the corny joke, the easy laugh, and those three little weather words that meant anything but "I love you"—scattered rain showers.

Frankly, I wanted to kill the man. I wanted to string him up from his radio tower with his microphone cord. I wanted to beat him senseless with a compact disk player. I wanted to shove a country western record up his nose. I wanted . . . I wanted . . . arrrrrgh!

Excuse me. Let me get a hold of myself. Before we get too far along in this little tale, I should explain the background a bit. Then, maybe you'll understand my feelings toward justifiable homicide directed toward a weather guy. I don't get this way that often. This guy just pushed me over the edge.

It all began as nothing more than a planned elk-hunting trip with Art Hobart, a bowhunting buddy of mine. We would be heading to the Missouri Breaks of Montana, prime elk and mule-deer country in the north-central part of Montana. It is as beautiful a piece of hunting country as you could find in this world. There are thousands and thousands of acres in the Missouri Breaks controlled by the federal Bureau of Land Management and the U.S. Fish and Wildlife Service. Mile after mile of the Breaks is public land, accessible on foot or four-wheel-drive vehicle to any hunter lucky enough to get there.

Part of the Breaks is made up of pine-covered hills and

deep, rugged coulees. Some of the rest is the cottonwood and willow forest of the river bottoms that straddle the Missouri River just above and on both sides of Fort Peck Reservoir. Finally, there is the sprawling sagebrush prairie, grasslands that once fueled the big herds of buffalo as they dotted the landscape.

In short, the Missouri Breaks is a big block of public land with a reputation for producing big elk, fine mule deer, antelope and upland birds. It's a place where you can see the stars at night without a single city light and darn few yard lights to blur your view. It's spectacularly wild country.

If there's a single problem with the Missouri Breaks as hunting country, however, it lies in the fact that it's far, far off the beaten—or let us say—paved path. Concrete or asphalt roads can be more than 50 miles away. Even gravel is a scarce commodity. What you mostly have is a mixture of hard-packed clay and bentonite, both of which can turn into greasy goo when it rains.

Both the good points and the bad points of hunting the Breaks were well-known to Art and me. We hunt the place often between the early days of September when the archery season begins and the close of the rifle season in late November, basing our operations out of a travel trailer that Art drags there during the season.

As we prepared for an October journey to the Breaks early in the big-game rifle season our mission was simple enough. We wanted to fill a cow elk tag that I drew.

A weekend was chosen. Long-range weather forecasts were consulted. And then our wives threw the first little wrinkle into the trip. They decided it would be nice to take our sons along.

In my case, that was 12-year-old Andy—old enough to hunt, but not licensed for bowhunting yet, but with enough energy to want to explore every square mile of the Breaks in just one weekend. In Art's case, it was his three-year-old son Mike—old enough to want to pack along plenty of toys, but not to accomplish anything in life unless it's done at full speed.

As for Art and me, we felt sure we could weather the company. After all, the Breaks were a big place and there were plenty of places for the kids to burn off steam. If we could just control their energies in the hours surrounding dawn and dusk, we'd have enough time to have a decent chance to hunt.

The long-range weather forecast for the weekend seemed to smile on us. There was no rain in the forecast. No early-season snows darkened the prospects for Saturday and Sunday. As of Monday and Tuesday and Wednesday, things looked great. A discouraging word or two did creep in on Thursday's forecast, as the television weatherman told us a storm might begin moving in late Sunday. But that wasn't too bad. After all, we were leaving right after work on Friday. It would still give us enough time for a good hunt and we could pull out ahead of the storm late Sunday afternoon.

It wasn't until we were actually on the road, making the 150-mile drive to the Breaks that we tuned in the car radio to the small northern Montana station with that the cheerful weatherman. With the two boys napping in the backseat, we first heard that those three little words, "scattered rain showers."

That's what the man said, amid jokes and cheerful chatter. North-central Montana would have scattered rain showers Saturday. In fact, it was 20-percent scattered rain showers. No big deal. I've heard about those 20-percent scattered rain showers before. Usually they're just a dark cloud or two. Those dark clouds might spit out a few drops. They might hit here and miss there. It wasn't a big deal. Usually, I told Art, the weatherman is just covering himself against possible failure when he says 20-percent. The 20-percent is used just in the off chance that a few drops might fall. Most often, it doesn't rain at all.

In this case, the first raindrops from those scattered rain showers began hitting the metal roof of Art's 23-foot travel trailer at about 4 A.M. Saturday morning. I remember waking up when they began their patter on the roof. I remember rolling over and thinking to myself that these few drops would pass. After all, they were only scattered rain showers.

The weatherman told us that was all they'd be.

At 5 A.M., when the alarm went off, I awakened again and listened to the rain on the roof again. Another passing shower? Hmmmm. The weather guy got his wish. He got the few drops to cover himself. So I rolled over again and fell back to sleep. No point in getting up until the rain quit.

I did the same thing at 6 A.M.

And the same at 7 A.M.

At 8 A.M., I joined the boys, who had awakened by that time to stalk the wily breakfast, and listened again to the steadily increasing pounding on the metal roof of the travel trailer.

Turning on the radio, Art and I heard the cheerful weather guy once more. He was sticking to his guns. This was, after all, just a scattered rain shower—in fact, just a 20-percent scattered rain shower.

Peeking out the window, I saw the results of the scattered shower were already making puddles out in the sagebrush.

The bentonite clay soil was deeply cut by the tread of Art's boots when he went outside to get something out of the truck. And the rivulets running down nearby hills meant the ground had already soaked up whatever it was going to take of this scattered rain.

Meanwhile, having successfully stalked the wild breakfast, the natives in the trailer were already starting to get restless.

You just don't cage a 12-year-old boy, much less a three-year-old. They were already bouncing on the beds. They were rough-housing with pillows. They were looking for chandeliers to swing from. And I think they were trying to figure out how to run a four-minute mile using the narrow path down the middle of the trailer.

As the day went on, the rain continued. So did the boys. And the trailer steadily began to shrink in size around us as Art and I cowered in our respective corners trying to stay out of the path of reckless youth. It got smaller and smaller and smaller being filled with kids who became more and more active as they sought to burn off energy. I thought Art described it amazingly well when he said that by the end of that day, his 23-foot travel trailer had shrunk to the proportions of an outhouse.

We had no place to hide. And still the 20-percent scattered rain showers continued. In all, that scattered shower packed rain for 18 straight hours before dropping off to a 20-percent scattered rain drizzle. All the while, we were held prisoner inside the trailer, being the terrorized victims, of the energy boys—the 12-year-old looking for a universal gym and basketball court and the three-year-old who laughed at anything he figured was silly—which was everything—and who defied anything that remotely resembled taking a nap.

Even when the rain did quit Saturday night, it didn't really help us. In its wake on Sunday morning, we found the rain had turned the clay and bentonite into an endless sea of gumbo goo that made almost any outside activity impossible.

Mud caked on the bottom of shoes and boots so that you couldn't walk, much less run. The wind was raw. The air was damp. The day was dreadfully cold.

Art and I took his four-wheel-drive out into the world of

mud and cold that day anyway. I know we shouldn't have done it—and it all turned out just fine—but we left the 12-year-old watching the three-year-old for a while and took off for a quick slip-and-slide up the road.

We had to go. It was for our sanity. When I looked at Art, I was pretty sure he had already lost all his sanity during the previous day's rain-forced captivity in the trailer with the kids. From the way he looked at me, I think he figured I had suffered the same fate.

It was on that muddy run up the road that we ran into the two hunters from Havre, Montana, who had been lured into the Breaks by the same forecast. They had heard the same radio weatherman Friday night and his predictions of scattered rain showers, too. And, while they were stuck in the less-than-luxurious confines of a tent all day Saturday because of it, they had come up with some solutions for the weatherman problem.

"Let's kill him," one said with a smile.

"Let's string him up from his radio tower," chimed in the other with glee.

"Yes, yes," we agreed. "Or, better yet, let's strip him naked and put him outside in his scattered rain showers. He'll chap and his skin will wrinkle him to death."

Aside from any humanitarian or legal considerations, it sounded like a great idea to us. We'd even buy the rope. The hunters from Havre were still chuckling with diabolical delight when they drove off, sending up sprays of water and clods of mud skyward as they headed for the highway.

We were less happy as we headed back for the trailer, hoping to find it still in one piece when we got there. We had to face the children again, and try to get their energies directed toward packing gear for the long ride home.

No, there was no elk or deer hunting that weekend. There was no peace and relaxation before heading back to work the following day, either. All of it was drowned in the scattered rain showers and buried deep in the gumbo mud of the Breaks.

As we drove home with both boys asleep in the back seat, we talked more about our plans for the radio weatherman.

I'll admit our thoughts in his direction were harsh. We felt no mercy after what we'd been through. And even murder began to sound like too easy a way out for the man of the quick wit, the corny joke, the cheerful voice and the frighteningly errant forecast. Finally, we thought of a better way.

We'd be nice to the man. We'd invite the weatherman to go hunting with us the next time the weather forecast began to turn gloomy. When that time came, we'd lure him to Art's trailer for the weekend. We'd provide all the food and entertainment he could handle. We'd greet him at the door. We'd cheerfully invite him in. But when that radio weatherman stepped inside, we'd rush outside and quickly lock the door behind him with the two boys already waiting in the travel trailer to keep him company.

Then we wouldn't let him out for two straight days, no matter what the weather might bring or how much he screamed for mercy. It seemed like the perfect thing to do after the horrors his forecast had inflicted on our beautiful weekend of hunting. After all, a man in his line of work should know what life in the Missouri Breaks is like when the weatherman is all wrong.

And he ought to know that no matter how much you like your kids, your sanity is extremely tested—and usually lost—when you're confined to an outhouse with them while the weather guy makes a mistake and cheerily forecasts those three little words—scattered ... rain ... showers.

DAVY CROCKETT!

Hats off to the sheep hunters. For all the many types of hunters out there—those who stalk deer and elk, those who call in ducks and geese, or those who chase upland birds and turkeys—I can tell you that sheep hunters are different. They're a special breed all their own. I know their passion well.

I got interested in bighorn sheep to add a little adventure to my life and introduce some bigger challenges to my hunting. I'd been hunting big game in my home state of Montana since I was a kid, going after mule deer, pronghorn antelope, mountain goats, bighorn sheep, black bear and elk. I'd chased white-tailed deer some, too, but there really weren't that many of them around in Montana when I was growing up. There are a lot more now.

Bighorn sheep presented a mountain hunt that would take me to the highest and wildest of places in Big Sky Country. You had to be in good shape physically. You had to climb and stalk over difficult terrain. You had to be able to shoot well, know your rifle well and gauge your distances to present a perfect shot. You had to be intimate with a wildlife species that is often extremely tough to find and can be hard to get close to even after you do find them.

My hunting partner, Keith Wheat, and I decided those challenges would be just perfect for us. So we hooked up with Bob Kahle, who knew a lot about bighorn sheep hunting, and began our learning process in the Spanish Peaks, south of Bozeman. Keith and I knew the country pretty well already from all the other hunting we had done there. And, we made some dry runs early in the season, looking for sheep but not finding any.

It was late in the fall when we finally got some fresh snow

on the ground to help us along. We went to the Dudley Creek area one foggy morning and began our climb up the creek bottom toward sheep country. We were probably halfway up the drainage when we began hearing sheep talking to each other. It sounded like there were a lot of sheep. We couldn't see them. They were shrouded in that fog. But we didn't dare move any further for fear we'd scare them off.

The Cow Decoy

Gordon Eastman was a great outdoor filmmaker and a good friend of mine. We had a lot of fun together shooting film of hunts in Montana and Wyoming. But there was one hunt that never quite made the film stage. It involved the cow decoy.

I was archery hunting at the time and we found a good bunch of antelope, including some big bucks that were spread out among a herd of Angus cattle. How were we going to get close enough for me to get a shot and for Gordon to catch it on film?

A plan was hatched whereby we went to town and got a big, stiff, piece of two-inch-thick Styrofoam. We began turning that Styrofoam into a cow. We drew out the design with some ears, a mouth, a nose. We had a glass eye, which we were really proud of. That eye would make it look real. And we found a piece of black cloth to cover it. Finally, we cut a hole out of the center that I could look through and a place to get a grip on the decoy. I also had a stick along to prop up the decoy for when I wanted to shoot.

With the stage set, we returned to the field with the antelope and the Angus, and I started my sneak. That's when things started to go wrong. For one thing, there was a big wind blowing and it was all I could do to hang onto the decoy, much less try to prop it up with a stick. The herd of Angus cattle turned out to be a herd of Angus bulls and they really perked up when that new Angus of mine showed up. You might call it love at first sight. So the bulls started running toward me and came to within 25 yards, then skidded to a stop. The running bulls started the antelope running in the opposite direction. The antelope didn't like me at all. And there I was, holding the object of the bulls' affection for dear life in that wind, for fear if it let it go, it would turn into a giant black cow kite. Then I'd be left alone for the bulls to do with me what they chose.

Slowly, I backed off toward a fence and eventually made it to safety. When I got back to where Gordon was set up with the camera, I asked him if he got any good footage of that. "Don," he said, "I was laughing so hard, I never even turned on the camera."

So we sat down and listened and waited for the fog to lift.

There's a certain wild mystery that settles all around you when you sit on a fogged-in mountainside. You can hear the sounds, but can't tell exactly where they're coming from. Sometimes they sounded close. Other times they're further away. Were the sheep moving? Were they staying put? All we could do is wait for the morning fog to lift in order to find out.

The fog eventually did burn off and we could see the bighorn sheep. It was a huge herd of them—by actual count, about 120 in all. But it was mostly a herd of ewes and lambs. Only a couple small rams were with them. Where were the bigger rams?

As we glassed the surrounding terrain, we saw some tracks in the snow further up the drainage, far behind and above the band of lambs and ewes. Could that be where the bigger rams were?

It took us a couple more hours of working up the mountainside to reach the place where we saw those tracks. We marked the spot with a little clearing and used that as our reference point as we picked our way up the slope. When we got there, it looked like a single set of ram tracks, bigger and heavier than the tracks left by the ewes down below. We started following them as they went up the mountain. When we got into the timber, the tracks suddenly split. It was actually three sheep moving ahead of us—the last two stepping into the prints of the leader as they went along. Once in the timber, they spread out. In the clearings, the tracks would come together again into that single line.

Our path finally took us to a series of cliffs and finally to a little ledge, perhaps six inches to a foot wide, that skirted one of the very steep slopes. The sheep had walked on that little ledge, then jumped up about three feet to a wider ledge that led to a more level and open spot up ahead. I was in the lead and inched my way along the narrow ledge, finally getting to a point where I could peek around into that level spot. There, I spotted a half-curl ram on a rock pillar, looking right at me—just 25 yards away. I ducked my head back down and told Keith that the ram was right in front of me. I couldn't see the other rams, but they were likely bedded down right there with him. How were we going to get a shot at them?

The only possible action was to somehow get to that upper ledge. The sheep had jumped up there easily. But Keith and I weren't sheep and we already knew that bighorns could go places where man simply couldn't follow. We formulated a plan—not a great plan—but a plan. There was a tree up above that I could just barely reach with one hand and, by using that as leverage, I could swing myself onto that upper ledge. Keith would then have to grab my legs and swing himself up. If we were lucky, we wouldn't spook the half-curl ram we knew was there. If we were really lucky, the other two rams would be bigger and we might each get a shot at one. There wasn't much real estate for all this to happen, however, before the sheep would disappear.

We executed the first part of the plan perfectly—we got up on the ledge. But then the little sheep saw us and he took off running. The other sheep spooked, too. Both were good rams. Both were moving fast. At the last possible moment, Keith and I each got a shot off and both sheep disappeared. When we walked to the spot where we last saw the sheep, we saw two deep ravines that dropped perhaps a thousand feet into the creek bottom. Keith's sheep appeared to have skidded down one of them. Mine went down the other. Picking our way down each of the ravines, we found that they came together down at the bottom. When we reached that point, there were both sheep. Both were dead. They were stacked on top of one another. Both were a sheep hunter's dream. Mine was just big enough to make it into the Boone and Crockett Record Book. Keith's was smaller—it was still an eight or nine year old ram—but didn't make the book.

That was enough to get me hooked on sheep for life. I set personal goals of taking bighorns out of different drainages in the part of Montana where I live. I took a number of them over the years. I helped guide other hunters to bighorn sheep. And I took my love of sheep hunting on the road to hunt the wild places of dall sheep in Alaska and stone sheep in British Columbia. I always had to make those hunts on a shoestring budget—that's the reality for many sheep hunters who are also raising families. They were hunts to remember.

Just as I hoped when I made the decision to hunt bighorns in the first place, sheep hunting has taken me to the highest and wildest of places. Just as Keith and I wound up tip-toeing on that narrow, little ledge in the Spanish Peaks in search of our first bighorns, other sheep hunts over the years would test stamina and determination in sometimes greater ways. To me, that's what sets hard-core sheep hunters apart.

Perhaps the most demanding sheep hunt I was ever on came in British Columbia when I set my sights on stone sheep. Two friends and I flew commercial flights from Great Falls, Montana, to Calgary, Alberta, then into Dawson Creek, B.C. The outfitter then flew us in his plane to a distant gravel runway that was 100 miles southwest of Watson Lake. Then, finally, we flew in a smaller plane to a remote camp operated by Frank Cook at a place called Frog Lake. Once again, it was a budget hunting trip, one we figured to make on our own without the help of a guide. But we found out when we got there that we were required to have one. That guide turned out to be a young Indian boy who turned out to be my partner up on the mountain, while my two friends hunted together off in another direction.

This was truly wild country, marked by impenetrable brushy bottoms, ice-cold rivers and streams fed by high mountain snowmelt, steep, rocky slopes and broad vistas with peaks as far as the eye can see. Trails, where there were trails, were game trails and trappers' trails. Spike camps would be set up on gravel bars on the rivers. The climbs were long and tough to get to the mountaintops where the stone sheep would be. The Indian boy and I crested those mountains and began working and glassing the high basins over on the far side.

Finally, we spotted sheep—ewes and lambs. They weren't too skittish, just working their way along ahead of us. The Indian boy and I followed them. These stone sheep finally dropped out of sight behind a rock ledge below us, and I told the boy he should roll a rock down there to see if other sheep might be down there as well. He tossed a fist-sized rock. No, no, no, I told him, roll a big rock. So I got down and wedged my feet behind as big a boulder as I could move and pushed it loose. It gathered steam on the way down that steep slope, kicking up dirt, dislodging other rocks, creating a small-scale avalanche that crashed over the ledge and into the valley below.

It didn't take long before stone sheep started coming up out of there, including a group of five rams that scrambled up a distant ridge. The rams were pretty far away. Also, they were skittish, milling back and forth. Through my binoculars, it was tough to see which one was the biggest. Through the rifle scope, it was even tougher. The Indian boy asked for my binoculars and I gave them to him. Between us, we tried to pick out the biggest of those distant rams. I found a rock-solid rest for my rifle. It would be a long shot. When we finally decided on the biggest ram, I held high enough to adjust for the distance and I squeezed the trigger. I hit the ram on the first shot. I put another shell in the chamber and hit the sheep again. Down, the ram went.

"Davy Crockett!" the Indian boy exclaimed. He must have been the only American he knew who had a reputation of being a great shot in the wilderness. As for me, I was less concerned about my reputation and more concerned about how we were going to get that beautiful ram back to camp. After caping out the sheep and loading the meat into our backpacks, we had to make a decision on whether to climb back up over the top or drop down the drainage to the stream, follow that to the river and follow the river around the mountain back to camp. Downhill always sounds best—especially when you're packing a load. So that's the way the Indian boy and I headed.

It was plumb dark by the time we got to the river. We couldn't find a trail and the brush was impenetrable on both sides, so the only way we could go down the river was to get into the water. The stream was ice-cold, perhaps 10 to 20 feet wide, and moving pretty fast. As the night grew ever darker, we picked our way along with all that fresh sheep meat on our backs and visions of grizzly bears dancing in our heads.

It got even scarier when the stream started dropping into a canyon. The speed of the water picked up. It got deeper. All we could do is try to grab hand-holds on sheer rock walls on both sides of us. Up ahead, the river was getting louder. This wasn't going to work, I told the boy. We were going to have to go back. We'd have to go with the other plan—climb all the way back up the mountain and retrace our steps down the other side. With the help of the moonrise, we hiked back to the top of the mountain. I looked back and the river we were following dropped into a 200-foot waterfall past the rock canyon where we decided to quit the river.

The moonlight gave us a fix on a distant peak that marked the way home. We continued on and eventually hiked down the slope to the trail that would lead us to camp. By then, it was 4:30 A.M.

The Indian boy and I could see the glow of the campfire

ahead. I could see my two friends stretched out sleeping nearby. They had heard the shot and figured I might have had a sheep down that was going to take me a long time to pack out. They had sat by the fire waiting and worrying about our fate until they finally got tired and fell asleep.

Just before the Indian boy and I walked into camp, I gave out with my best imitation of a grizzly bear roar, growling and snarling and snapping. My sleeping friends shot out of their makeshift beds like rockets. They were grabbing for rifles and scrambling around until they finally saw us laughing at them.

All in all, it was quite an adventure—even for a veteran sheep hunter. And as to that grizzly bear growl that topped it all off, that wasn't too bad either. I don't know who could have done it better. Not even Davy Crockett.

WHAT, ME MISS?

S ometimes, the earth must momen-
tarily stop spinning on its axis.
Gravity must take a few-second
break. Ill winds must blow at odd
times. Invisible forces must tug or
push on us. How else can you explain why hunters miss the target?
How can you explain why they
sometimes miss it, then shoot and
miss it again, and sometimes again and again.

I'll admit it; I've missed. Sometimes, I've missed really
badly. And this despite the fact that I dutifully head to the
rifle range and never begin a hunting season without my
rifle being sighted in and my shotgun skills being brushed
up a bit.

In hunting, there are times when you do bump a rifle
scope and knock it off line. There are winds that blow. As to
the earth on its axis, gravity and invisible forces, I've used all
of those alibis, but they probably don't really happen.

At times, missing is just plain inexplicable.

One of my worst displays of hunting marksmanship actually came on a fishing trip. John Kremer and I were hiking
along the Boulder River in fall, bushwhacking our way
through a pine and alder forest toward a beaver pond that
held some nice brook trout. It was September and mountain
grouse season was open, so I packed along a .22 caliber revolver in case we saw a blue or ruffed grouse. It's legal in
Montana to hunt mountain grouse with pistols and rifles, as
well as shotguns.

Midway through the forest, a ruffed grouse flushed right
in front of us. There are places in this world where ruffed
grouse are post-graduate smart. They rocket out of thickets,
dodge through stands of trees and zoom out of shotgun
range in an instant. That is not the case with most ruffed

grouse in Montana. The old saying here goes that if you want to hit a flushed ruffed grouse on the wing, you'd better get it before it comes to the first available branch. Once it reaches that branch, it's going to land on it and sit there and look back at you. That's just what this grouse did.

John and the Whistle

John Kremer and I were like two lost souls who found each other as the perfect soul mates during the end of our college years. John was a dyed-in-the-wool trout fisherman who had prowled the creeks, streams and rivers. I had fished for many other species, but I'd never fished much for trout. I was a hunter who hit the thickets for grouse and sought the wily white-tailed deer. But John had never done any hunting. Any time we had a free day during our final years of school, we went fishing or hunting. During the spring and summer, I introduced John to warm water species, and he took me on trout streams. In winter, we had some tipups and went ice fishing. And in fall, I introduced him to bird and duck hunting.

Standing a fit 6 feet, 2 inches and long and strong of leg, John cruised the grouse and pheasant areas and never seemed to stop. I, with much shorter and rounder legs, took all my regular rest stops. But he had a problem. For one thing, he was pretty excited to be out there. For another, he kept forgetting what this was all about—carrying shotguns and hunting with them.

So on those first few pheasant and grouse trips, likely as not when a bird flushed, he'd point at it and say "There's one!" He'd never take a shot, or he'd take one when the bird was almost out of range. If I was close enough and the shot was safe, I'd pull the trigger and try to get it.

Finally, after a few trips like this, I came over to his house one evening and announced that I'd purchased him a gift. I'd given him a really nice silver whistle.

"Wow! That's nice," he said with a puzzled look on his face. "What's it for?"

"Well," I began, "This is for our next hunting trip together. When you flush a bird, just blow on this whistle, jump up and down and point in the direction the bird is going. If you're not going to shoot at them, the least you can do is make my hunting a little easier by alerting me that there's something I need to shoot."

I think John carried that whistle in his hunting vest for quite a while, but he never needed to blow it. He became a shooter at game and a hunter—a good one, too—and, in time, I became a pretty good trout fisherman.

It wasn't all that far away—maybe 20 feet. So I took the .22 revolver out of its holster and took dead aim, hoping for a quick, clean head shot so I wouldn't ruin any meat. Bang! The grouse still looked at me. Bang! Same thing. Bang! Bang! Bang! Bang! That meant my untrusty six-shooter was now empty. Yet the grouse was still there sitting on that branch looking at me, occasionally poking his head up a bit further, as if to tempt me.

"Perhaps you'd better reload," John said. "Maybe you can get him with the next volley." I went through the routine again—six shots, six misses—taking good aim each time. By now, John was laughing pretty hard after each shot. That didn't help my confidence any. As for the grouse, this ruffed was still unruffled.

"You might have a better chance of getting him if you just threw a rock," John said. "But you'd better have five more rocks handy. After all, you'd better have your rock magazine full before you start. And you might have to reload your rocks, too."

On the next reloading, I finally hit the branch the bird was sitting on. He flew about five more feet to another branch and lit on it. On the 17th shot, he finally flew off. And John laughed even more.

All right, so I wasn't a champion pistol shot going in. But 17 shots at 20 feet? Not even a bad pistol shot can be that bad. And then, the only way I can get the bird to move is by hitting the branch he's sitting on? Good grief! I wasn't even scaring him.

My buddy John used that incident for years to offset any good shooting I might perform. "Got your antelope in one shot, eh? You sure?" he would say. "Maybe somebody just told him about you and the grouse and the antelope died laughing."

Speaking of antelope, that's another species that can humble a hunter. Out on the wide-open prairies east the mountains, hunters get a good opportunity to discover how really good—or really bad—they are as shooters. I've done both. Often, I do make it a one-shot pronghorn season. But the difficulties of judging distance, prairie winds and the fact that pronghorn antelope really aren't that big of a target sometimes brings a shooter to his humble knees.

On one of my early antelope hunts in Montana, I was out with John Ramsey, who was a brand new game warden in Baker at the time. He arranged access for us to a huge ranch which was teeming with antelope. We'd drive slowly down the two-wheel tracks that served as roads on the ranch, stop and glass with binoculars. We located many antelope herds that way. Then we'd go after the antelope on foot, trying to put a sneak on them to get within range.

Antelope hunting is arguably the best hunt in Montana and can be as easy or as tough as you choose to make it. You always see antelope—unlike elk, which can be awfully tough to find. You get to devise intricate stalks over long distances, using every possible wrinkle in the landscape to hide yourself from the sharp eyes of the pronghorns. And when you get up on them, you have to make a decision as to whether the buck in the herd is big enough for you and you want to end the hunt right there or whether you want to find another herd and do it all over again in search of a bigger trophy.

John and I saw a lot of antelope on the ranch. Those herds included a lot of really nice bucks. We'd put a sneak on them, get within range and I'd shoot and miss. I'd shoot once and the herd would run away. I did it time, after time, after time. John was most polite and understanding. He never said a word, except to lift my spirits after each miss. He said it was fine, that we'd just find another herd.

After this grand display of bad shooting, we spotted a good-sized herd out on a big flat. There was just a little dome of ground that we could hide behind as we stalked within range. When we got to the dome, I slowly crawled to the top and settled my gun for a shot. Boom! Another miss. As the antelope raced to the right, I emptied my rifle in frustration at them. Four more shots. Four more misses.

I slumped down. I must have looked awfully dejected at that point. John said—and I still can't believe he said this— that I should just lie there quietly and he'd poke his head up and look around to see if there were more antelope out there. After all that shooting? What buck, doe or fawn in its right mind would still be around after that cannonading? John poked his head up a few inches, then quickly dropped back down.

"There's still an antelope out there. It's over there to our left," he said.

"A buck?" I asked.

"Yes, it's a buck," he answered.

"How far?" I asked.

"Only about 100 yards," he said.

As quickly as I could, I fumbled through my pockets for another rifle cartridge. I loaded that single round in the chamber of the rifle. Then I inched my way up to the top of the dome again. I couldn't believe it. There he was. It was a lone antelope buck, just standing there. He was looking at me dead on, showing me the front of his chest, neck and head.

I looked through the rifle scope one more time, took aim and squeezed the trigger. At the sound of the shot, the antelope dropped like a rock and didn't move at all. John patted me on the back and headed off toward the antelope. I ejected the spent cartridge, got up and followed him.

"Wow! That's some shooting," John said when he looked at the buck. "You hit him right between the eyes."

I looked down at my boots for a moment, rolled my eyes skyward for a moment, then came clean. "Yup, that's some shot all right," I told him. "Right between the eyes, eh? But I was aiming for the middle of his chest."

When I got back to town, I checked that rifle at the shooting range. Yes, it was shooting a little high. But from the chest to between the eyes? It wasn't shooting anywhere near that high. I blew the shot and just got lucky.

In other instances, you can explain away your poor shooting. Conditions are simply tough. That would describe days in a duck blind when the wind is high and the birds are riding that big blow at high speeds past you. I've had some of those. I've had days when the pheasants and grouse refused to hold and flushed far out in front of you at the very edge of your shooting range.

And there was the time when we found all the sharptails in a big patch of Ponderosa pines that led down a coulee in the Missouri Breaks. It was primarily a bowhunting trip for elk. But when Art Hobart, a friend from work, Terry Koper, a friend from Wisconsin, and I saw all the birds flushing, we grabbed our shotguns and went in to find them.

Shooting in that patch of pines was brutal. Some of the birds had landed in the trees. Some landed on the ground. It was thick enough that as soon as you heard a bird flush, you started looking in that direction and might get a quick glimpse of the grouse in small openings between the branches before it disappeared. It was snap shooting— quick, fast, exciting—and horrible for accuracy. I had blown about eight shotgun rounds at the birds without touching a single feather when Art started needling me about it.

"I thought you could shoot. All you do is blow holes in the air. The great shotgun shooter. You couldn't hit a sharptail if you tried," Art began. "In fact, if you hit a sharptail with your next shot, I'll even retrieve it for you."

"On all fours?" I asked.

"You bet!" he said.

"In your mouth," I asked.

"You bet, that, too," he said.

It was a deal. By that time, we'd pretty much run out of pines and run out of sharptails. The birds had scattered so far down the coulee that we never found them again. We went back to camp and had lunch. We went through the mid-day rest and relaxation period that bowhunters often enjoy between the early morning hunt and the evening hunt. While the morning hunt was often up in the timbered breaks and coulees, the evening hunt was on stands in the river bottoms and on the islands of the Missouri River.

On this day, Art had to run his boat from one river access point to another access point a couple of miles downstream. We planned to set out from the downstream spot and head to an island for the evening. So I drove the truck down to the first access and dropped Art and Terry off where the boat was pulled up on the riverbank. They headed down the river in the boat.

While I was driving the truck back through the hills toward the downstream access, a couple of sharptails flushed right next to the road and flew down a little coulee, landing in a small patch of juniper. Ah ha! These were just the birds I needed. I pulled the truck over, grabbed my shotgun and walked down the coulee toward the birds. When the first sharptail flushed, I took careful aim and dumped it. I never got a shot at the second bird.

When I arrived at the downstream access, Art and Terry were already there and talking to some other hunters. I nodded toward Terry, got him aside and whispered, "Grab your camera." When Terry was ready, I put the bird behind my back and walked up to Art with what must have been a most wicked smile.

"What do you want? And what are you smiling about?," Art said.

All I said was one word—"Fetch!"—and I tossed the bird out in front of him a fair distance.

"Oh, no!" Art said. But, true to his word, he got down on all fours and shuffled on his hands and knees toward the bird. He picked it up with his teeth and started shuffling back toward me. As he got closer, I kept backing up so Terry had plenty of time to take pictures. Finally, Art dropped the bird and got up, spitting loose feathers out of his mouth as he did so.

"I don't know how those dogs do it," he said, spitting again. "When I got that bird in my mouth, those feathers sucked out every bit of moisture I had in there. Bleccch! I don't know what dogs see in those birds. They don't taste that good to me."

Only then did Art pause to ask me, "You really got that bird on the first shot after all those misses?" I assured him I had. It was at least a mildly humiliating moment for Art, especially in front of those other hunters. But it wasn't nearly as bad as when he got to work on the following Monday. I'd blown up and copied one of the pictures that Terry took and plastered it all over the office. Everybody had a good laugh, even Art.

The lesson is simple. No matter how hard you try to prevent it, missing sometimes happens, no matter what you're hunting. The important thing is to practice, practice, practice. Then take extra special care to make the shot good when you've got a bet on the line.

GET 'EM STARTED RIGHT

K ids! They're one of the greatest joys in the outdoors. They're also one of the biggest worries. They can be a giant frustration. And, most of the time, they just flat amaze you with what they do, don't do, and how they seem able to explain it all away in just a few words.

My wife Dee and I had four children— Wade, Kirk, Lori and Ryan. As you might imagine, they all took their turns in learning about such things as fishing, hiking, hunting, camping, skiing and all the other aspects of Montana life in the mountains. And while each of them had their moments, the eldest—Wade—was the one who had the first whack at educating his father about taking kids into the outdoors. Did I learn everything there was to know? Hardly! Each of my children taught me something new. Even now, that education continues with grandchildren. But at least Wade got me started out right in dealing with kids in the outdoors. And, in the end, I got Wade and my other children started out right, too.

The parents' creed for taking children into the outdoors: Be prepared. Be more prepared. Finally, don't expect any of your preparations to turn out exactly as you planned. For example, take the candy bar incident.

Wade may have been 10 years old at the time. He might have been younger. But he was to join me, my friend Mark Wright, my brother Doug, and Doug's son Russ on a fishing trip into the high country. The plan was to backpack in and stop and camp at various fishing spots along the way.

Wade was the smallest of the bunch, but he still wanted very much to be a part of it. If we were carrying backpacks, he wanted to carry a backpack. So I got him a little bitty one and strapped it on him. As to his load, I thought about that for a while. How about the candy bars? There were five of us and we planned on being out for five days. Figure a candy bar apiece for the adults each day and two for each kid each day. That made a 35-candy-bar total, just about the perfect load for a little boy.

The three adults took the lead as we headed down the trail, then Russ, then Wade. It would be a four-mile hike into Diamond Lake, our first night destination. The first two-and-a-half miles of the trail was pretty much level. We'd have to climb for the last mile-and-a-half. The going was pretty good at the start. By the time we hit the three-mile mark, it was time to stop and take a break. Wade was lagging behind at this point, just following the trail behind us. We watched him come up to meet us.

When Wade sat down, I told him that this would be a pretty good time to break out a candy bar for each of us. Wade answered, "Well…" and then looked down. Puzzled, I looked into his backpack and found it was empty. "What

happened to the candy bars?" I asked him. "Russ ate the last one," he said. Russ ate the last one? I couldn't believe it. In three miles of trail, Wade had devoured 34 candy bars. And Russ got the last one. No wonder Wade lagged so far behind. It took time to take that backpack off 34 times and unwrap 34 candy bars. At least he learned the value of carrying a light pack.

How Wade escaped a giant bellyache, I don't know. But he didn't seem too much the worse for wear as the party hiked on. Wade would score another first the following day. Along the trail, we found a nice little stream running into a lake. He caught his first fish—a nice little cutthroat trout—on a fly rod from that stream. In those mountain streams, it's often easy pickings for cutthroats. Trout don't see too many fishermen, so they aren't real wary of fishermen's flies. And often there are so many little trout in the stream that they're always competing for food. They're always hungry. You just drop a fly in and they come up and take it.

Wade was pretty excited. I was pretty proud, too. So it was time to haul out the camera and take some snapshots of the occasion. Wade squeezed that trout so hard during the photo session that its eyes bugged out. I told him we had to keep it and that it would make a nice addition to supper that evening. So he caught a couple more.

When we got to the camp spot on the second night, I volunteered to set up camp because everyone else wanted to go fishing. I kept Wade nearby, sending him to a little creek that cut through the meadow where we were camping. It was such a little creek, that we had jumped across it on the way to camp. But we saw some trout scatter when we jumped, so I knew there were fish in there.

My instructions to Wade were pretty simple: I told him to go to the creek and see if he could catch some fish for supper to go along with the ones the others would catch. I took my time setting up the tents, leveled the place off, pulled some rocks in so we could sit around the fire that evening. I could see Wade fishing away down on the little creek.

Finally, I wandered over to see how my young fisherman

was doing. "Did you catch any?" I asked him. His answer was, "Twenty-three. I've got them all over here." Twenty-three? Five people? How hungry did he think we were? And how many trout would the others bring back? We had to eat them. We couldn't keep them fresh while we were hiking around in the mountains. Let's just say we ate trout that night until they stuck out of our ears.

As Wade got a little older, I was able to take him hunting with me. Living in Gardiner, Montana, in the heart of good elk country, we didn't need to travel far to go hunting. Often we'd go up into the mountains after school and go archery hunting for elk. It took almost no time to get to the hunting area. We'd have a few hours of daylight and then the prime time of sundown. It was perfect.

One such trip was made with my friend Rod Churchwell. Wade, Rod and I hiked up onto a ridge about two miles into the backcountry. The plan was to spread out and hunt the ridge down to our vehicle.

I told Wade to go down the top of the ridge. I'd break off on one side a bit and work down through the timber. Rod took another path that would take him to the open meadow near the vehicle. It should take us about an hour to get down there. We would arrive together just before dark. It was the perfect evening hunt. So we split up and began working down the slope.

I got down to the park first. Not too long afterward, Rod hiked in. We waited for Wade. And waited. And waited. No Wade. Finally, we began hollering for him, but heard no response. Finally, I climbed back up the ridge to where I left him. Still no Wade. Where in the heck did he go? He might have taken the wrong ridge. Another option was that he hurt himself. Or, maybe got attacked by a bear—after all, this was grizzly country.

I knew Wade had his fanny pack with some matches and all the other goodies in it that you need to pack when you take a trip into the mountains. But still, it was tough to keep a parent's imagination from running wild. If there's a possible disaster that could find a path through your mind, an incident like this one is guaranteed to put it there—and let it grow.

Rod and I finally drove to town with a plan to call all our buddies, put together a search plan and go back up and find him. By then, it was about 9 P.M. Finding friends willing to

The Porcupine Adventure

Once upon a time, the college in Bozeman, Montana, needed some live porcupines for a research project. I knew because I saw an ad in the local paper saying just that and offering $50 for every live porcupine that someone would bring them.

It wasn't exactly a get-rich-quick scheme, but I told my uncle that I knew an area that had a pile of porcupines. If we figured out how to get them, we might make ourselves a little money.

Our plan was to track them in the fresh snow until we found them up a tree. Then one of us could climb up the tree after them, put a noose around them, and lower the porky to the other guy who would put it in a gunnysack.

We found out right away that this plan didn't work very well. But we also found out you could herd porcupines about wherever you wanted them to go. If you climbed above them in the tree and pushed them a bit with a stick, they'd climb back down the tree. The guy on the ground would then hold them down with another stick. Then you could push them into the gunnysack.

We got pretty good at it by the sixth porcupine. We were already counting our money. When we got back to town, I called the college researcher and told him what we had. He told me to just bring them over. When we got there, he asked where we had the porcupines and I told him they were in the gunnysacks. He thought we were joking. But he got his cages and we started dumping them out.

When the researcher saw them, he was reluctant to pay. But we said they were, indeed, live porcupines, which is what he asked for, and he finally agreed to give us the $300.

The biggest lesson both for the researcher and us that day was that you can trap live porcupines, but you'd better not transport them in gunnysacks. Very quickly, a gunnysack will pull all the quills out of a porcupine. Those porkies we delivered looked like they had been plucked. And when you take all their quills off, what you're left with is a porcupine that looks like a little, bald, pink rat.

I haven't tried to capture any porcupines since.

mount a search party was the easy part. The hardest part was telling my wife Dee that her son was lost and we can't find him. You know how mothers are—they sort of go into hysterics. If you think your imagination can run wild, let a mother's imagination begin churning. They think of things 10 times worse than any man would think of.

After we got Dee settled down a bit, we were ready to return for the search. There were six of us and we broke up into parties of two. At night, sound carries real well. We figured to split up to fan across the mountain side, go up a ways, holler a lot and periodically fire a pistol and hopefully hear Wade yell back.

The route for my partner and I was the furthest ridge he could have taken by mistake. It wasn't a pretty route. There was a creek and solid deadfall, marshy ground, no game trails. We'd fight our way for a while, then I'd holler and listen for an answer. I'd go up a bit and holler some more. Finally I got to about a mile from where I had last seen Wade. I hollered and heard a little voice up above in response. I hollered again. Wade hollered back. What a relief!

I got up to where the sound was coming from and there he was on a hillside above the creek. Wade had a fire going. He had a pine bough bed he was lying on. He had simply holed up in the darkness and was waiting for daylight. It was the best thing he could have done. From his experiences with me, he knew what to do. We had talked about getting lost and what you should do and shouldn't do. He was doing just that.

When I finally got to him, it was 4:30 in the morning. The first thing he said was "What took you so long?" It was one of those frustrating moments of fatherhood. You wanted to shake him until his teeth rattled. You wanted to hug him tight and never let go. A full range of emotions washed through me. Emotions take over. In the end, you're happy and relieved that he was found and wasn't hurt. Not everyone who gets lost in the mountains winds up that way.

I pulled out my pistol and shot up in the air three times to let the others know we found him. That was our signal. We waited there and everybody came back in. On the way home, we had a good talk about how Wade handled himself. We had agreed he had done it all right—except for getting lost in the first place. As for his mother, you can't imagine how she felt. It was breaking daylight by the time we got home.

Get 'em started right and these youngsters will turn out to be very capable outdoorsmen. That's not to say there won't be some bumps along the way. But all in all, they'll be the best partners you'll ever have.

WALLEYE FISHING FOLLIES

I t was really quite an honor. I was asked to be the featured speaker at the annual banquet of the Glasgow, Montana, Chapter of Walleyes Unlim-ited. Me, a wall-eye speaker. Wow!

I was pretty excited that my friend Alton Smith would even ask. After all, I've had something of a checkered past in my walleye fishing. No one has ever called me Mr. Walleye, though I like to fish for them a lot. Actually, I like to fish for everything a lot. Nobody has called me Mr. Trout, Mr. Pike, Mr. Bass or even Mr. Sucker—though that last entry is a lot closer to what people call me. In this case, walleyes have been a particular passion of mine in recent years after three decades of rising through the ranks of Montana trout fishing with bait, lures and finally flies, wet and dry, big and small, feathered and furred.

Walleyes were a new, yet very old, challenge for me. I'd grown up fishing for bass, walleyes, northern pike and muskies with my dad back in Wisconsin. But when I moved to Montana after college, I was going to make the most out of the prime trout country that filled so much of my new state. So I fished trout on creeks, streams and blue-ribbon rivers. I learned new things and grew in my skills until I could both talk the talk and walk the walk in trout country.

As the rivers and streams became more crowded, I began looking to walleyes again. Walleye waters in Montana are generally big reservoirs. You could climb into a boat, rev up the outboard and leave the crowds behind as you found some secluded spot. Besides, walleye fishing had changed. There was so much new and delightful gear I could gather. Boats were plumb full of high tech gadgets and gizmos.

There was a new learning curve of fish-finders, electric trolling motors, western reservoir strategy, nifty rods, reels and lures and lots of other neat stuff that we didn't have back in my younger days. Finally, all this learning and investments in all the gadgets and gizmos was being rewarded with a major speaking engagement.

"So what do you want me to talk about?" I asked Alton. "Should I tell them everything I know about walleye fishing?"

"No," he replied. "We need the talk to run more than two or three minutes. You are supposed to be the main speaker."

"How about telling them about how to use all those gadgets and gizmos in your boat to really home in on the walleyes," I asked him.

"No," he replied. "I can see from watching you out on the water that you haven't figured too much of that stuff out yet."

"Fishing fashion?" I asked.

"You kidding?" he answered.

I was rapidly running out of speech topics.

I think I saw him stifling a giggle when he said, "How about your tournament fishing? That ought to be real interesting." He walked away, rounded a corner and the laughter finally exploded.

Tournament fishing, eh? Yes, I had fished assorted Montana walleye tournaments over the past decade. But as I thought about it, there wasn't much enlightenment that I could offer the walleye crowd at the banquet from my experiences. Or was there?

When the night of the banquet arrived and I walked to the podium, I began by telling them that I was one of the few fishermen that everyone else is happy to see at a tournament. They know, for sure, that I'm not only never going to win it, I'm not even going to place. Some fishermen are contenders. I'm a donator. While others contend for cash and prizes, my entry fees always go into somebody else's pockets. I donate them without ever a hope for a return. That makes other tournament fishermen happy.

There was a one-day tournament once that my son Matt

and I threatened to win—sort of. Along about mid-morning, I felt a strong bite on the jig and minnow at the end of my line. I set the hook and was instantly embroiled in a ferocious fight with a fish. For five minutes, I battled him, and he battled me, while Matt stood at the ready with the landing net. Finally, the fish came up from the depths.

"It's a carp, Dad," Matt said.

"No, no, no, Matt. It's a golden walleye. It must be a 15-pounder," I replied.

"Big rubbery lips, sucker mouth, big scales, a few whiskers, it's a carp," Matt said.

"Well, you may think it's a carp now," I told him. "But at the weigh-in at the end of the day, I'm going to call it a golden walleye and see how it goes. I'll bet nobody else caught a 15-pounder today. I'll finally win something.

There was some logic to this. After a long, hot, dry day on the water, beer usually flowed pretty well by the time the weigh-in began back at the marina. If I just dawdled around long enough and was one of the last fishermen to bring in my fish, maybe the weigh master would have downed enough beer that his vision would be a little blurry and he'd buy my golden walleye tale.

Matt balked. He said he'd come to the weigh-in with a paper sack over his head. He wouldn't even cut eyeholes. He didn't want anyone to be able to identify him as the son of the "golden walleye fisherman." Reluctantly, I threw the carp back in the lake.

The banquet crowd seemed a little wide-eyed at this. They were looking at me. But their mouths seemed to hang open a bit in disbelief at what they were hearing. But maybe, just maybe, they were actually really impressed.

So I continued, telling them that after a number of tournaments like this one, I had adopted a new strategy. If I was going to be a donator and wasn't going to win or place in these things, at least I would make my presence known. You do this by making a spectacle of yourself in front of as large a crowd as possible. Take the Jordan/Hell Creek Tournament a few years back.

Matt was in the truck as my boat backer at the launch

ramp on the first morning of the tournament. I was in the boat, waiting in a line that seemed to stretch on forever as 137 boats were taking their turns at the ramp. When it was our turn, Matt backed the boat in, I fired up the motor and then putted out to the middle of the bay while Matt parked the truck and trailer.

With other tourney boats all around me, I went about the tasks of getting ready for the day. I pulled out rods and reels. I checked the bait. I glanced around and noticed the boat seemed to be riding a little bit low in the water, but that was just a passing thought. I got all the electronics plugged in and working. Geez, this boat seems to be riding low in the water. I packed away the lunch and pulled out the life jackets for our run out onto Fort Peck Lake. Hmmm . . . wow, it's low . . . and why is that boat plug sitting there in the splash, well . . . shouldn't it be in the boat?

"Sinking! Sinking! My boat is sinking!"

I meant to say it under my breath—cool and calm. But I must not have been cool, calm or saying it under my breath because boaters all around me began laughing.

The water hadn't seeped up through the floor yet, but without that plug in, the boat was taking on water fast. With 136 other boats bobbing around out there watching, I got the motor going and plowed the water-logged boat toward shore, running it right up on the bank as far as I could. I turned on the bilge pump and the water began pouring out. Matt came back, waded in the lake and put the plug in the boat. The bilge kept pumping. He then walked back to camp to change his wet clothes. The bilge kept pumping. Tourney time arrived and the other 136 boats began the long, one-by-one procession out past the start boat. The bilge kept pumping. Matt walked back. All the other 136 boats were now out and fishing somewhere. The bilge pumped a while longer, then finally quit.

By the time our boat got out past the starting line, the official start boat was already back at the marina. The official starter and his crew waved at us over their coffee cups and breakfast as we finally headed toward our fishing spots. At least we didn't have to battle other boats to get out of the bay that day. We had a clear run out onto the lake all to ourselves. Best of all, it gave the echoes of laughter from the other boats ample time to fade away.

That happened several years ago. But I still can't go to a boat ramp anywhere without somebody asking me if I remembered to put the plug in my boat today. Or was I going to make them laugh like I had during the tournament when I was out there hollering, "Sinking! Sinking! My boat is sinking!"

The banquet crowd still seemed to have that wide-eyed, awestruck look on its face. Wow! They must be in awe. I must be telling them real-life tournament strategies they've never heard before. So I continued on.

The scene was the Montana Governor's Cup Walleye Tournament, the biggest tourney in the state, held out of Fort Peck Marina. Instead of 137 boats in the field, this tournament had 200. There was such a line at the boat ramp in the morning that Army Reservists were directing traffic. Instead of one truck backing a boat down the ramp at a time, they were running two and sometimes three boats down the ramp simultaneously.

Dan Majeske was my partner. It was his boat and he remembered to put in the boat plug—after laughing at me one more time over my Hell Creek "Sinking! Sinking! My boat is sinking!" My job this day was to back his truck and boat trailer down the ramp and launch him. He'd be in the boat.

Dan's pickup truck is a huge diesel—much bigger than my little pickup. His boat trailer is a big, tandem-axle affair—also much bigger than mine. Let's just say there are reasons why Matt does the back-the-boat-down-the-ramp on our fishing trips together.

When it was our turn, however, I found that big, rumbling diesel engine was indeed my best friend. Over the sound of that diesel, I could barely hear Dan screaming, "Sign! Sign! You're going to hit the sign!" I pulled ahead and started over again. This time, once again, I could barely hear "Outhouse! Outhouse! You're going to hit the outhouse!" I pulled ahead again and started backing down again. This time, Dan was loud and clear, "GAS PUMP! GAS PUMP! YOU'RE GOING

TO HIT THE GAS PUMP!!!"

In front of all those folks and the Army reserve, Dan climbed out of the boat and took over at the wheel of the truck. He quickly backed the boat straight down the ramp and into the water. Then he climbed into the boat as I walked down and meekly said, "I think I can pull the truck straight up the ramp and park it. I think I can . . . I think I can."

Fishing the Governor's Cup was an adventure as well. Fishing had been so good in the days leading up to the tournament. People were catching big walleyes. They were catching lots of them. Even I caught a few. But while others caught fish during the tournament as well, Dan and I had our troubles—especially me.

As in all fishing, the key is to find out the pattern that's working. You locate the depth where the fish are holding. You discover the bait or lure they like best. You fish the bait or lure at the proper speed to trigger bites. If you only find

that consistent pattern and then stick with it, you'll catch a lot of fish. But we couldn't find a pattern, no matter what we did.

First, we looked for a pattern with the fish and found none. We tried different offerings at different speeds and those patterns didn't come together either. Finding a pattern with the fish was a dismal failure. So we looked elsewhere for clues to a good tournament catch.

We did hook and land a keeper walleye once where there was a herd of cattle on the shoreline. So we looked for other herds of cattle. But there weren't many other herds on the shore that day and the ones we found didn't produce. At that, I found a kindred soul. Somebody in the banquet audience sadly nodded his head. He said that he, too, had caught a walleye near a herd of cattle in that tournament and looked in vain for other hot herds without finding them.

We caught a little walleye soon after I opened up a can of Diet Pepsi and took a sip. A couple sips later we hit another small walleye. I nursed that can of soda pop for the next hour in hopes of it becoming our can of plenty. By the end of the hour, it was pretty warm and tasted pretty flat. But worse than that, we didn't get another single bite.

Finally, we caught another keeper. This one hit while Dan, who had consumed quite a few cans of pop himself in the boat that day, was doing what people do when they drink too many liquids. I pondered the pattern of catching a fish while he was doing that. I really put the cans of pop and bottles of water to him in hopes we could get more keeper walleyes. If Dan's bladder only cooperated, we might get a limit yet. But that pattern didn't hold up either.

I tried staring at our fishing lines. I tried ignoring them. I tried burying myself in the cooler looking for a sandwich and pouring myself a cup of coffee. That usually works, but it didn't work this day. For Dan, who often cashes winning checks at tournaments, it was a sad tourney performance indeed. For me, I was just a donator again—a familiar place for me to be.

But when the tournament was over, people came up to

me, patted me on the back, and thanked me for that great show on the boat ramp. Watching me go through that, it simply took the pressure off them completely. They were able to settle their tournament nerves with a good laugh that carried them to successful days on the water. Whenever they got worried about their fishing, they just thought of me on the ramp again and realized there were others who could do worse.

I finished up my speech with solid advice that the members of the audience could become a welcome sight on tournament day for their competitors, too, and could do much to boost the spirits of others. They, too, could follow my creed of being a donator of entry fees, rather than a winner of prizes.

Of course, they might have some difficulty locating future tournament partners, unless they had a family member willing to submit to sharing time with them in the boat.

All they had to do to become a donator was be a not-very-good fisherman, try sinking their boat a time or two, threaten a gas pump on the boat ramp, and spend their fishing days looking for herds of cattle on the shoreline. In the end, if they only did these things, they might even catch a big golden walleye.

ADVENTURES ON SKIS

Many of my friends think I'm an iron man when it comes to cruising the mountain trails in the spring, summer and fall. That, of course, is the kind way they put it. These days, they call me a "mountain goat—an old mountain goat—but a mountain goat nevertheless." In some ways, I guess I am. I love to hit the trail to the high country, get a steady and comfortable pace to my step, and go see what's on the far sides of mountains. There's always something new to see on the other side.

Over the years, I've enjoyed doing the same thing in winter with cross-country skis. But I'll be the first one to tell you that the cold season and deep snows makes for a whole different set of rules and problems. And being a far traveler—going a ways beyond the places most people go—makes for some unique adventures, as well. You'd better be prepared for whatever Mother Nature throws at you.

Here's a little tale to illustrate what I mean.

Rod Churchwell and I were going to ski from Cooke City, Montana, down through the Lake Abundance area, spend the night there, and then head on down Slough Creek, stay overnight at the ranger's cabin at Frenchy Meadow and head out from there. A game warden and Dave Morton, the local forest ranger, were going to use snowmobiles, head up Slough Creek, and meet us at the cabin. It sounded simple enough.

Things went as planned and we hooked up with the game warden and Dave at Frenchy Meadow. By the time we got there, both Rod and I were pooped. It had been a long trip on skis. Rod opted to ride the snowmobiles out, but those snowmobiles had made a fine trail down the creek. I figured it wasn't all that far, so I'd just ski my way out.

I started down the trail and it was great skiing. It was a bit further than I thought it was, but that was all right. Then I ran into the herd of moose.

Down at the end of the meadow, there stood 10 wintering bull moose. Moose are not what you hope to run into on the trail at any time of the year. They look big, ponderous and slow. But in truth, they're one heck of a lot more agile than a man on cross-country skis. They're also darn unpredictable. They might let you pass. They might not.

I'd heard tales of bull moose treeing a man—and no, I really didn't want to think about climbing a tree with skis—and then sticking around the area, chasing him back up the tree every time he tried to come down. Cow moose with calves are even worse. Of all the deer species, they're certainly the most aggressive when they want to be.

The snowmobiles had zipped right past the moose without a thought. But there I stood. The short winter day was already beginning to come to a close. It was getting dark. I skied up to about 50 yards away from the closest moose and got my flashlight out and started flashing the light at him. He didn't budge a bit. He just looked at me. I certainly didn't want to test my luck, get past that first bull, and find myself in the middle of the moose herd.

All I could do was backtrack on the snowmobile path, then abandon the good skiing and get out into the fresh snow and make a big circle around the 10 bulls. It took a long time and I wound up skiing along the creek itself, working my way slowly along, trying to get back to the path. Meanwhile, my friends couldn't figure out what happened to me. They finally came looking for me and eventually found me skiing through the deep snow.

In an effort to help me along, they said they'd pull me back to camp with a snowmobile. That turned out not to be such a good idea. They threw me a rope and hooked it up to the snowmobile. I lasted maybe a hundred yards before I piled up into a tangle of skis in the snow. I wound up skiing out under my own power—and at my own pace.

For people who have never spent much time in the mountains in winter, it's hard to describe how different things are. Winter comes early to the high country with the first snows in September and the last snowfalls lingering on into April and May. Cold can be severe. Mountain snowpack is just that—snows packed incredibly deep in most years. And if you get far off the beaten path, you're just that—far off the beaten path and on your own.

The best way to describe it is with a trip I made with Dave in the middle of winter. We planned be out overnight and go into Shooting Star Lake from the Cinnabar side. It was an area we both knew well from hikes there in the summer.

This time, we planned to go in with skis and backpacks with our overnight gear up a fork of Cinnabar Creek. When you cross-country ski uphill with a backpack, it's a little like plain walking. Coming down is more like skiing. Going up is the hard part. Coming down is easy.

Low clouds and fog had settled in on the morning we left. That often happens in the mountain valleys of winter. It limits your long-range visibility and, at times, you can't even see short range very well. Deep snow also covers the trails and even the blaze marks on trees that mark it. But what the heck, we knew the way. We'd been there so often before. So off we went up the drainage, making the only tracks in a beautiful unbroken expanse of snow.

We skied and we skied in those low clouds, working our way toward our destination on the top of the divide. Finally, the clouds burned off as they also often do by the middle of mid-winter, mountain mornings. We looked back down the slope and were surprised to see a set of tracks down below going through an open park. We put the binoculars on them and then it dawned on us. Those were our tracks. We had skied up one side the drainage, circled the end without going to the top and were now on the opposite side heading back. Lots of skiing done, but not much progress made.

Dave and I headed back in the right direction and made our way to the top of the divide. Up there, the snow was well over 10 feet deep. Among the things the snow covered was all available firewood. To cook dinner, we had to have firewood. It was a must. To turn dinner from dry, crunchy, dehydrated stuff, we also had to have water.

I told Dave that I had put in an old bighorn sheep hunting camp in the area and with it, there was a good stack of firewood next to a tree. Near the camp, there was a high-country spring that fed a little stream of cold, clear water. All I had to do was find the camp.

That turned out to be not much of a problem. We found the camp, found the tree and used the back end of our skis to dig through the deep snow. There was our firewood. Now, we needed the water. We skied the short distance and dug through the 10-plus feet of snow again. This time, however, things didn't go so well. The spring was bone dry. How could that happen? Well, many of these high-country springs are fed by snow melting up above them. The snow melts. The water soaks into the ground. The spring of snowmelt emerges—unless, of course, the whole world around it is frozen like it was during this trip.

We gathered up snow and got our snow-melting pots going. That provided the water. We enjoyed our dinner. With breakfast the following morning due to rely once again on water to turn dehydrated food into something palatable, Dave had an idea. He had an aluminum Army canteen with him in a canvas case. He figured to fill it with water and keep it in his sleeping bag with him overnight. Our water problems the following morning would be solved.

Dave and I camped on the snow that night. All in all, it was a cozy camp. The temperature did drop pretty low that long winter night, as it always does in the darkness at this time of year. The wind blew some. By the time we awakened, we were hungry for the blueberries and oatmeal that would be heated for breakfast. So Dave reached for the canteen. The water inside was frozen solid—even though it spent the night in his sleeping bag. That gives you an idea of how cold it gets even inside a sleeping bag on a mid-winter night in the high country.

Here's one last tale to illustrate how different the world of winter is in the high country. This involved an ice-fishing trip with my friend Mark Wright.

Our goal was to ski into Hidden Lake in the Buffalo Creek drainage. It involved a lot of upslope travel, but we felt the goal was worth it. We skied across Slough Creek, which was frozen, and then we went up to Buffalo Creek. The snow, when we got there, was about 12 feet deep.

We skied up to the lake. I had packed along an axe head, which we planned to strap to a small lodgepole and use it to chip our way through the ice. We guessed the ice might be a foot or two deep. We broke through and hit water. We poked the pole down further and encountered another layer of ice. The pole we were using was about 10 feet long. The way those mountain lakes freeze is you have a layer of ice, then a layer of slush, then a layer of ice, then a layer of slush and then more ice.

Finally, we were down the length of the pole and pushed it down and figured we were down through the ice layers and into the body of the lake. We baited our lines and dropped

The Tote Goat

The mountains of Montana are big, big country. Roads are not to be found everywhere. As a result, we got Hernandez, our Mexican donkey, to help us penetrate the high country. I've used my friends' horses. And Keith Wheat and I were among the earliest people in this area to invest in what were called Tote Goats.

Tote Goats were a miniature motorcycle built out of steel tubing, tires, a seat and a Briggs and Stratton motor—not much more. They weren't fast. They weren't fancy. But they were pretty darn durable. You could climb hills, bounce along trails and, in the process, scout a lot of this big, big country for hunting and fishing.

If the Tote Goat didn't get you all the way into a high mountain lake, it at least got you within hiking distance. And that's what Keith and I did during the summer.

On this particular trip, we were going to Tote Goat in to Deadman Lake. We had our fishing gear, our auxiliary gas cans and the Tote Goats.

What I had failed to recall, however, was that I had made a recent trip to Billings to trade off an old Mercury automobile for another vehicle. That old Mercury was prone to vapor locks in its fuel pump during the heat of the summer. And the quickest way to clear the vapor lock was to pour cold water onto the fuel pump.

When it came time to make the trip, I couldn't find a container to hold the cold water I needed. But my one-gallon auxiliary gas can for the Tote Goat was empty. So I used it. On the drive to Billings, a vapor lock stopped me cold. So I dumped about half of the cold water I had along on it. The vapor lock cleared and I drove on.

Time passed between trading off the Mercury and our Tote Goat trip to Deadman Lake. I filled up the auxiliary gas can before I left town, forgetting that the can was half-full of water. And, sure as heck, my Tote Goat ran out of gas far into the backcountry. No problem, I thought. I just filled it up out of the gas can.

The Tote Goat ran about 100 yards, then stopped. I pulled on the starter rope until my arm was sore and couldn't get it started again. It took long enough pulling on that rope that I remembered why it wouldn't start.

At that point, there was nothing I could do. Keith figured he'd help me out by pulling me down the trail with his Tote Goat. That worked for a brief time. Keith seemed to think that fast was good in this towing situation. I was using hand brakes, foot brakes, everything I could to keep my Tote Goat under control.

After a few wrecks, I finally decided to simply push it down the trail. Which is what I did—a long, slow, push back to civilization. No matter how easy you try to make it going into the backcountry, you've always got the hard way—your feet and legs—to take you back home.

There's really no moral to this tale. It's just a tale, as so many of them are in this book. Except if you read between the lines, you'll notice among these tales that whether it's a high mountain donkey, a kid who eats all the candy bars, a bald porcupine or a man in waders being chased by a moose, there are always great plans that don't quite work out, sudden adventures that tickle your funny bone, and a whole lot of fun to add to your memories of the outdoors. Enjoy them all. Your own tales will warm your heart and make you chuckle for a lifetime—long after your legs carry you home from the outdoors.

them down and began fishing. We fished. And we fished. We fished all day long. We never had a bite.

I finally told Mark that I thought we might still not be all the way through the ice layers. I got a longer pole and pushed it down, and sure enough, there was more ice.

At that, we gave up on it. We knew there were big fish in that lake. We thought we were going to have a great day. But as it was, after cutting through 10 feet, we had spent the whole day fishing between ice layers.

On the way out, we found a herd of elk tucked in a small place amid the deep snow in that high drainage. Snows were piled so deep all around them and the terrain was such that you knew they'd have to spend the entire winter there. They could paw down for just enough grass. They had just enough room in that little area to move around. And there they stayed, waiting for spring to free them. Truly amazing.

The lesson is that the world of winter in the high country is a different kind of place for both man and beast. It poses some great adventures on skis for finding your way around, navigating the terrain, making your camp, even for fishing. It's a harsh environment. But one well worth exploring.

THE PVC TREE

T rees are only for squirrels and nuts. I might add, some of the squirrels you find up there are definitely nuttier than others. Before you get the impression that this is just going to be a little nature talk, I should explain that what we're really discussing here are trees as they relate to tree stands and nuts and squirrels (who are the tree stand hunters).

Talk to enough tree stand hunters and you'll find they always turn out to be squirrels and nuts. They may not start out that way, but they always end up that way. How do I know? In the end, it's the tree stand that turns into the final objective rather than the hunting opportunities it provides. It's the tree stand itself that has magical and mystical properties that defy all logic and override all other factors related to the sanctity of life and the safety of limb.

For example, you'll find the old standard of being 10 feet above the ground on a deer stand has changed. It used to be that 10 feet was enough. Deer didn't look up. If you got 10 feet up a tree, you were in the clear for deer spotting you. But that's changed. It's at least 15 feet now, and the really magic number has become 20 feet. Just get yourself 20 feet up in the air and deer and elk will beat a path to your tree. Can 25 feet up be far away? How about 30 feet? Give a hunter an oxygen mask and who knows how high he'd climb.

Aside from my concerns about air sickness and the fact man wasn't blessed with wings, the main problem with this strategy is that hunters will do anything to get themselves up there, regardless of whether it's logical or safe. They may balk at using a sturdy ladder on a level floor to get something for their wife from a high shelf. Overhead light bulbs might remain burned out and hunters will grope in the dark of a room for weeks. But nothing is too flimsy when it comes to getting up that tree to hunt. And no tree is too flimsy to hold them as they sit up there with their oxygen masks.

One friend of mine used a combination of sticks, twine and two limber saplings to get up in an elk hunting tree stand. It was a precarious climb at best. Once he got up there, the tree was so flimsy that he and his stand literally swayed in the wind. Taking a steady aim from that position would have been a miracle.

Another time, the same friend found a big, old, dead tree to set his stand in. A week before the hunting opener he mounted his portable tree stand there—solid—and figured he was all ready for the first day of the season. He walked into the area in the pre-dawn darkness that opening day and figured he had gotten himself turned around because he couldn't find the tree. He walked around and around, peering up

into the gathering light in the eastern sky, looking for the silhouette of that portable stand. Finally, he stumbled over it. During the week, a wind had blown through and the old, dead tree had toppled over. His stand was still firmly attached—solid—but the tree lay at his feet on the ground.

Yet another hunter I know had his self-climbing tree stand turn into a speeding elevator, racing toward ground floor, as its grab on the tree failed and the stand raced down the tree at gravity speed against his will. Truly a moving and eye-opening experience, until he hit the ground.

And yet another friend looked on with dismay when a ladder he had used to climb the tree blew down, leaving him with a clinging, scratching, and scrambling descent of the tree at quitting time. All in all, an abrasive situation.

That's when my hunting partner Art Hobart came up with his big plan—the PVC Tree. The PVC Tree grew out of one of those between-season discussions where alcohol wasn't present, but probably should have been. Alcohol, at least, would have provided an alibi for Art's fantasy. Instead, the PVC Tree took root one day at work during a planning season for the upcoming elk-hunting season.

Art had spent many years playing the squirrel and nut game high in the branches of dead cottonwood trees and skinny aspens. He had even taken a six-point bull elk that way.

"Next year, I'm going to take in my own tree," he began. "No more putting in a tree stand only to have someone else use it when I'm not there. No more having other hunters put in their tree stands close by, scaring all the elk away or cutting them off before they get to me. No more having stands in the wrong place with no way to move them quickly and easily. I'm going to make my own tree this year. I'm going to make it out of a 16-inch PVC pipe and set it up where I want it!"

"Oh yeah? Really? A PVC Tree?" I burst out laughing. "What are you going to do," I asked him. "Plant a one-inch pipeling and wait for it grow?"

"No, really, I'm going to put a base on it like a Christmas tree, extend the legs out three or four feet. I'm going to cut steps in it so I can climb it easily up to about 15 feet—maybe 20 or 25," Art said.

"Three or four-foot legs, eh? Then you're going to climb up one side to 15 or 20 feet? That should make a nice crash when you topple backwards into the brush."

Undaunted, he gathered steam on the project, getting more and more excited about it as he went along.

"I can drag it in wherever I want—whether there are any trees there or not—and set it up where the elk are moving. Everybody else will be stuck in his tree, and I'll have the only portable tree around. I'll be all by myself."

"Oh sure, you'll lug this big pipe around back in the brush, all by yourself. The only part of that I believe is that you will be all by yourself. No other hunter would be able to hold back their laughter if they were within a half-mile of you."

"I'm going to cut it out on one side so I can sit back into it," Art said "That way, I'll be hidden until the elk come by. It will be a perfect ambush."

"Let's see, you're six-foot-two and over 200 pounds and you're going to sit inside that 16-inch pipe? Maybe at birth you could sit in that pipe. But not now, sonny, not now."

"The best thing about that pipe is that it will blend in perfectly with those old, bleached cottonwoods," he said. "Instead of woodland camouflage or Trebark camo, I can wear one of those gray flannel suits of underwear and wool socks."

"I can see it all now. You sitting up there in your underwear and socks for all to see. What a sight! A better camouflage would be to dress yourself up as a plumber. Then you could put a 'Men at Work' sign at the bottom and not an elk in the world would think you're hunting up there."

"I'll need to give myself some elbow room up there, so I can come to full draw. I'll cut out some holes for my elbows," Art said. "I'll put the seat on a swivel, so I can shoot in all directions."

"The swivel's great, but why bother with coming to full draw. Why not stay in tune with the theme and just whirl around and harpoon the elk with a plumber's helper. What a story to tell the other guys! You can say you harpooned a six-point bull with a plumber's helper in your underwear. You plunged him at 20 yards. You can even say you flushed him out without even using Drano. Your partner was the Liquid Plumber. And you field dressed that bull with a Roto-Rooter. All from your PVC Tree. Let Outdoor Life Magazine top that one!"

My friend Art was bloodied, but not beaten in the exchange. I was still bent over in laughter when he vowed to continue with his plans for the new tree stand and would, in fact, show me my folly when he shot an elk out of it the following fall.

All I told him was that I wanted to be there to see the unveiling and to watch him climb into position in that getup of his. It would, I told him, open up a whole new category of tree stand hunters for me. And I wanted my camera. I just had to have a camera to catch all this on film. If I didn't have the photos, nobody would believe me when I told them about it.

I could see it all now. While I kept to my own strategy of sticking close to the ground and dropping to my knees when game was near, he would be up there in his sewer in the sky. No longer would the trees be limited to the squirrels and nuts. Now, there'd be poets up there, too.

"Poets?," he asked.

"You bet. You remember the old verse you learned back in school, don't you? You know, that old Joyce Kilmer poem about trees? Now we've got the new and updated Art version:

I think that I shall never see,
A thing as strange as a PVC Tree.
Complete with a man high up in the air,
Who crashed to earth in his underwear......"

THANK YOU TO PARTNERS

As we said early on in this book, as outdoorsmen, we are products of all the mentors who taught us along the way and the partners who shared our fishing trips, camps, hunting trails and other ventures into the outdoors.

For all of us, these are people who are near and dear and play more important roles in our lives than they ever realize. My dad, like many dads, was one of the partners who started me on the right trail. There were many others along the way. But how do you really thank them for all they've done? It isn't easy.

One such person for me was Frank Martin, of Lewistown. Frank was one the few outdoorsmen I could accurately describe as a man for all seasons. Each time of the year brought something different in the outdoors for him.

Frank would hunt wild mushrooms in the spring and set up his photo blind to take pictures of displaying ruffed grouse and sage grouse. In summer, he'd cut his stacks of wood in the forest so they could dry for the fireplace in fall and winter. He could fly fish for trout and work Lindy rigs for walleyes with equal ease. Come fall, he'd harvest wild berries and make his own wine. He'd hunt birds and big game and was equally adept with shotgun, rifle and bow and arrow. Grouse, pheasants, deer, antelope, turkeys and the occasional elk hunt would all take their turn. And in winter, he'd ice fish, call coyotes and set the occasional trap for furbearers. On top of it all, he was schooled in wildlife biology so he could tell you about all the birds, bugs, animals and fish. Plus, he knew all the good spots to go.

Once, when he was in his truck and was leading me, in my truck, down a dusty summer road toward a distant small reservoir where he'd caught trout as big as a nine-pound rainbow and a five-pound cutthroat on flies, he pulled to a stop, got out and walked back to talk to me.

"Normally," Frank said, "This is where we put the blind-folds on people so we can keep the secret of where this spot is. But seeing as you're driving, I guess the blindfold is out." Then he walked back to his truck, chuckling all the way.

Another time, in fall, he took me to a huge rattlesnake denning area that was honeycombed with holes in the ground. "Listen to this," he said, and then he stamped his foot on the ground. The earth beneath us just buzzed with rattling snakes. "The last guy I took here was pretty deaf," he said. "Usually you can hear these snakes before you see them. He was impressed with the area, but he was pretty much scared to death, too."

Frank's eyes would light up when he told me about great hunts or fishing trips. His smile would grow broad. We relished the time we spent together and our evening chats when we came back to his home in Lewistown and enjoyed the sumptuous dinners his wife Betty would have waiting for us.

Finally, we were on a fishing trip together for walleyes and were taking a mid-day break in his travel trailer, when I tried to thank him for his friendship, our time together and especially for all the things he taught me. I stammered a bit. I couldn't quite find the words. I must have sounded pretty corny. But I went on and on about how great it was that he knew so much and had shared that knowledge with me on so many things.

"Well!" Frank said finally, in a serious tone. "After all that, I guess this must be our last trip together. I've taught you everything I know. You know it all now. So good bye."

Then he smiled. And we went back out fishing again.

ABOUT THE AUTHORS

In addition to sitting short in the saddle in the high country every chance he gets, Don Laubach is the founder and president of E.L.K., Inc. He is the inventor and patent holder of several game calls including the "Cow Talk" call, the first patented cow elk call made available to the public. More recently, he developed the universal coyote call, the "Yote Buster," and the "Power Howler." Don has co-authored *Elk Talk, The Elk Hunter, Deer Talk, Elk Tactics* and *The Coyote Hunter.* Laubach also was involved in creating a number of successful videos with legendary filmmaker Gordon Eastman and has more recently began creating outdoor videos on his own on elk, deer, coyotes and other game animals. All are available from E.L.K., Inc., P.O. Box 85, Gardiner, MT, 59030.

When Mark Henckel isn't terrorizing boat ramps, stumbling in streams after trout or sharpening his marksmanship skills, he is the outdoor editor of the Billings (Montana) Gazette. In addition to co-authoring *Elk Talk, The Elk Hunter, Deer Talk, Elk Tactics* and *The Coyote Hunter,* Henckel also wrote *A Hunter's Guide to Montana* and has authored six children's books on the outdoors as well. He has won national awards for his newspaper and magazine writing and has received a number of other honors from conservation and outdoor organizations. Henckel lives in Park City, Montana.

OTHER BOOKS FROM
E.L.K., INC.

Elk Talk
Your Guide to Finding Elk, Calling Elk, and Hunting Elk with a Rifle, Bow and Arrow, or Camera

The Elk Hunter
The Ultimate Source Book on Elk and Elk Hunting from Past to Present, for the Beginning and Expert Alike

Deer Talk
Your Guide to Finding, Calling, and Hunting Mule Deer and Whitetails, with Rifle, Bow, or Camera

Elk Tactics
Advanced Stategy for Hunting and Calling Elk

The Coyote Hunter
Tips, Tactics and Techniques for Hunting and Managing the Perfect Predator

For product information, orders, or free catalog, call toll-free E.L.K., Inc., 1-800-272-4355. Visa and MasterCard accepted. Web site: www.elkinc.com.
E-mail: info@elkinc.com.
P.O. Box 85, Gardiner, MT 59030